LEADERS INSIDE OUT

A Navy SEAL's Challenge To
Successfully Lead, Inspire, And
Motivate Yourself and Others
Every Day

Copyright

This manual contains material protected under International and Federal Copyright Laws and Treaties. Any unauthorized reprint or use of this material in any form is prohibited.

First Edition January 2018

© 2018 - Rob Robertson - All Rights Reserved

Limits of Liability / Disclaimer of Warranty:

The author and publisher of this book and the accompanying materials have used their best efforts in preparing this program. The author and publisher make no representation or warranties with respect to the accuracy, applicability, fitness, or completeness of the contents of this program. They disclaim any warranties (expressed or implied), merchantability, or fitness for any particular purpose. The author and publisher shall in no event be held liable for any loss or other damages, including but not limited to special, incidental, consequential, or other damages. As always, the advice of a competent legal, tax, accounting or other professional should be sought.

"Given to my wife and loving daughters... from a husband and father raised in part by a robber, a thief, a drunk, and eventually a man of amazing faith."

Would You Like To Get In Touch With Rob?

If you'd like to:

- Schedule a leadership coaching session

- Inquire about having Rob speak to your company or organization

- Or just drop Rob a note with your thoughts about the book and how it helped you

Please visit www.LeadersInsideOut.com Today

Table of Contents

Background and Biography

Rob grew up in California in a working class family. After graduating high school Rob enlisted in the United States Navy. Rob served the vast majority of his career in Special Operations.

Experience:

- 21 years in the navy

- 20 years in the navy SEAL Teams

- Served 12 years as an enlisted SEAL Operator Red Cell & DEVGRU included

- Served 8 years as a Chief Warrant Officer

- 15 additional years as an instructor and mentor for a multitude of tactical teams, foreign and domestic.

Titles & Awards

- 1990 CINCLANTFLT Sea Activity Sailor of the Year

- SEAL Team(s) Senior Training Department Head

- Professional Military Education Instructor for NCO Development

Personal Info:

- Founder of SEAL Quest Challenge for training and Leadership Development

- Sponsors young men at his home in Kitty Hawk, NC for mentoring

- Definitely a proud father

- *Interesting fact:* during one of his first night free fall parachute jumps he ended up tangled in high voltage electrical wires in Australia!

Rob sees his earned opportunities and ability to lead as a gift. He, like many others, started life with difficult beginnings. He relied upon his intuition for discipline to encourage, motivate, and improve himself. As he traveled through the ranks of the military, his participation as both a Follower and a Leader gave him great insight into the role of the authentic Leader.

From such experience and leadership roles he has mentored a multitude of young men, most of whom came from the Spec Ops community. Today he continues to make a difference by helping to shape and positively influence the lives of those who want to improve themselves and produce better results. Rob constantly strives to help others identify the Leader on the inside for the purpose of leading others from the outside.

Foreword

My name is Hershel Benton Davis. I started out in the United States Navy in the 1960s as a submariner. I was trained as a nuke, but then I got picked up and sent off to school. I volunteered for UDT training in 1965, went through Class 36, East Coast. Served in Underwater Demolition Team 21, served in Vietnam in SEAL Team 2 in 1969. So I wasn't one of the first SEALs in Vietnam. I was probably one of the latter ones.

When I came back from Vietnam, I went back to SEAL Team 2. I made Chief while I was in Vietnam. Then they were talking about pulling some of us SEALs out because too many of us were Chiefs, and so we said we should go to shore duty. I ran off to shore duty, and then that's when I wound up on the West Coast after a tour of shore duty and recruiting. There I was the Command Master Chief of Underwater Demolition Team 12. After a tour at 12, I was the Chief on the Navy Parachute Team and then moved to Underwater Team 11 as Command Master Chief. That's where I met Robbie.

Sometime around '81 to '83 we got re-designated SEAL Team 5 and Robbie was there at Team 5, but then he went off to Red Cell.

Initially, Robbie didn't stand out, which is not a bad thing in the Teams. He was just one of the boys. But when the skipper called me in and said, "I want you to take over training cell," I said, "Skipper, I'm the Command Master Chief. I don't want to take over training cell." He said, "You're one of two combat veterans I've got besides myself, and I want you in the training cell. If you'll do the training cell for me too, you can pick who you want." I said, "Now, that sounds like a deal!"

For those of you who don't know, as SEALs we train all the time. We'd go to the desert (among other places) every year and run ops. Being in the teams was training constantly. You're always going somewhere. You're deployed 80% of the time. If you're not going somewhere, you're somewhere in the States, going to school or out in the desert. You always got something going.

Mr. O'Connell, Naval Academy graduate, was the Officer in Charge of the training cell. Initially, he and I were a little bit at odds, but eventually he compromised and he got his land, I got mine. That's always good. Robbie was one of the deals. I just really liked him right off. I don't even know why I was there, because I'd say, "Robbie, here. Look here. Let's get this done!" There was a leading petty officer, but Robbie wasn't the leading petty officer. I think he was a second class petty officer, E5 in those days.

I'd say, "Robbie, blah, blah, blah," and he'd go, "It's already done, Master Chief." I'd say, "What about so-and-so we need?" "It's done, Master Chief." "Well, do we have the right equipment?" "It's all done, Master Chief."

That's when I started thinking, "Well, damn. What the Sam Hill am I doing here? This guy could do it by himself." But it just went that way, and I really have always liked him. I initially liked him primarily because of his loyalty, his ethical behavior, he was a good Christian man, and he had honor. Unfortunately, that's not always the case in a SEAL Team. Few men are born with the ability to exceed the sum of their parts, to be synergistic, Robbie is one of those in spades. His abilities had me scratching my head and wondering "Am I mentoring him or is he mentoring me?" In my career, I have learned a lot from those junior in rank to me.

George S. Patton's leadership principles, principles of leadership, would be something I had on my desk forever. Patton was my hero. I'm a Navy guy, but I like the way Patton did it. Staffing your weaknesses, that's what he called leadership. Staffing your weaknesses, if you're man enough, honorable enough, to admit you have some. Robbie was definitely one of my staffed weaknesses. God knows I had them like everybody else does. But unfortunately, in a SEAL Team with big egos and a lot of narcissism, many members think they're perfect. They think they can do anything. About 35% of them are that way, in my opinion. Of course, you need ego for what we do, but save it for the battlefield.

That's another reason why Robbie started to emerge, for me at least, as one of the finest examples of a leader I ever saw in the teams. You could always count on him, he was loyal, and he never made any excuse. There aren't many like that. There were a few. I can remember those guys too, but Robbie's loyalty is what stands out to me. That's a very rare commodity in this day and age. It's a dying art. It's all me, me, me. There's not a narcissistic bone in that boy's body. He's a giver, not a taker.

I'm sure he made mistakes, but when he was called on them, he never made any excuses. Actually, looking back, I can't ever remember calling him out on anything! We've worked a little bit now in the civilian world after he's retired, and he still exhibits the exact same leadership qualities at all times. His ethical behavior, he's honest, forthright, leads from the front, and that's what I call a good leader. If you're going to ask them to do it, you'd better be able to do it yourself and do it damn well... and that is what Robbie does!

If you want to learn about leadership, there is no finer example of a practical leader that I know of and I've really enjoyed watching him grow over the years. He started out as an "E nothing" and retired from the Navy as a Warrant Officer.

Another important trait Robbie has always exhibited is that he just always listened well. That's part of it too. He considered me his mentor, and he wanted to emulate me. Very flattering, I thought. Whether working with elite teams of special operators, or mentoring young men still in high school who want to serve our country, Robbie is so good at just leading and mentoring. Inspiring people to want to be and do their best in any situation.

I was, frankly, flattered when Robbie asked me to write this foreword. And when I read the book I realized it was going to be something special. Unlike the guys who beat their chests and say "Look at me and how great I am!" Robbie admits his shortcomings. He's honest. He's almost honest to a fault. Not that that's a fault, but he's just honest and he admits when he makes a mistake, and he fails forward. That's always been my key thing. It's okay to make mistakes. It's okay to make errors in judgment in my world as long as you learn from them and you fail forward. If you don't, then you're stupid. And over the years I've found there's only one surefire cure for stupid, and that's to turn off that fools birthday! (Well, maybe you can change stupid through religious conversion, but that's not really a debate we need to have here.)

If you want to be a better leader, a better person, and a better follower of people who actually deserve to be followed, read this book from cover to cover. It'll make you laugh, it'll make you cry, and it'll make you think. But most of all it will give you knowledge and insight from one of the most authentic leaders I've ever had the privilege to know.

Hershel B. Davis, USN, MCPO (Ret. SEAL)

Introduction

I swore to myself it must be something more than a style or a process. I wanted to know for myself what I was looking for when discovering and choosing the leader at various times in my life. What was I searching for when trying to figure out who could be this person, and how do they ultimately reveal themselves?

From leaders we get leadership, but this may commonly be associated with "management" and I've never seen those things as similar. I certainly see their essential relationship, but I wanted the personality not the process. I describe the leader in this book as "wise" or "discerning" because there have been plenty of humans we call leaders that have proven to be destructive. Aside from position or title, I wanted to know what to follow and how to find it, but I couldn't find it unless I knew what I was looking for. And, I certainly didn't know how to find and follow what I was looking for if I didn't first figure out how to lead myself.

Starting from the inside and decidedly working outward towards my leadership role in the SEAL Teams must have started long before the Teams. With regard to the Special Operations community my title was Chief Warrant Officer, the title didn't make me a leader any more than being a navy SEAL did. It placed me in the environment where I could experience and learn from a number of available leaders; regardless of their title, the choice for me to wisely follow remained voluntary. I would never have gotten anywhere without leaders willing to mentor and demonstrate the right expectations. There were plenty of them; I certainly wouldn't have been much without them… thank you!

Having come up through the ranks, enlisted to officer, I've had the pleasure of being a part of many lives. Each year that passed gave me a better understanding of people and leadership. I believe the leader is the one who has been given a sense in their personality for doing the "right thing" – no strings attached. With that statement I've just eliminated many politicians… you're welcome! I needed to see for myself the principled characteristics leaders demonstrate regarding the circumstance and the people they've been given, not the style of management they prefer. Leaders optimize performance from others by demonstration, because this is very much a requirement of their personality.

From the beginning I needed individuals to demonstrate the leader's role specifically related to who and what they were charged to care for; yes, I was in search of a performance. I saw firsthand the wisdom, experience, and knowledge of those placed into the leader's role. And though there were flaws, because they are imperfect human vessels, they possess an unwillingness to succumb to circumstance or condition. They have the capacity to see beyond the general observation and make the most of, or improve any situation by virtue of who they are in this life as a person.

I have never shared much of my personal life with others. I have no idea why, other than it seemed rather unnecessary and I have been given to keep these things private most of my life. I learned much about myself while recollecting from memory earlier life events. I simply closed life chapters to start new ones… so I turned much of it off. I needed this information to discover what I was looking for so I turned it back on… but the switch stayed off for a very long time and I was good with it. However, how was I going to understand my path to becoming a leader and for what reasons did this life role appeal to me? Why was I strangely unwilling to allow earlier circumstances to prevent my personality from emerging? Whatever positive personality characteristics I had, apparently they were willing to stay for the journey. Looking back, I see a recurring pattern where all I needed to do was put myself in the right place for the right reason while forcing each opportunity, through diligence and hard work, to produce the best result. In short, I was driven to seize every opportunity to do and be more in my life.

I've never met a leader who says they're tired of leading, and this book is an extension of that effort. Jim Edwards, the friend who encouraged me to write this book, once said to me, "Wouldn't you like to give a copy of your own book of leadership lessons to people who come to your course?"

John "Sully" Sullivan and I run SEAL Quest Challenge. People come from different parts of the world, different beginnings, differing social conditions, but they all come to personally challenge themselves. Many who come are leaders already. Some come because their emerging leaders, and some come because they're searching for leaders. I relate to all of them, but most closely to the last group because I know the journey. Much of what we do is a demonstrable affirmation of what we have come to experience regarding many things; the first of which I pray is leadership.

I want anyone who chooses to read this book to believe you are never limited by the version of life you've been given; you're only limited by the version of life you accept. I could only change or improve my version of life by exercising a determination and a will to earnestly and positively design it… that has always, and will always, belong to me. In reading this, I most assuredly hope for those interested and those searching, they become the leader on the outside once they discover and nurture the leader from within.

CWO Rob Robertson, USN Ret., SEAL

Chapter 1
What Is "Leadership?"

I've heard leadership and leader defined, we probably have all read or listened too much regarding the subject. Many of those definitions are quite good and helpful, but a definition is not a description, and I wanted to find the level just underneath the skin of our many definitions. I want to discover what it is we're actually looking at when we see this person we call a "leader."

What is the appearance of leadership? Our pursuit of leadership is an industry; in many was it is a commodity. We regard it as a virtue but, unlike many other virtues, we don't spend money on those the way we do for this one. Just Google the annual money spent on Leadership Development and Training and you'll see it is in the billions. Why? We are perpetually seeking leadership; we are forever pursuing good leadership values. Google the money spent on honesty, loyalty, or trustworthiness - or any other redeemable virtue – and you'll see no one pays for those. Why? These characteristics are the ones we expect leaders to have.

Wise leadership appears to be Mount Everest; we rightfully presume it is the all-encompassing mountain of virtue. Big money is spent trying to find or educate the perfectly balanced leading individual. We somehow understand the "ideal" model we want, but the actual production of that leadership requires an investment of time, effort, and commitment.

From personal experience I have had the pleasure of observing and participating in the leadership role on many occasions. I began my career in the SEAL community as enlisted and worked my way to Chief Warrant Officer upon retiring. Though I will relate several stories from my time in special operations, this is not a book about Navy SEALs. I want to describe leadership as I experienced it. Within my leadership roles and observations there was a lot of ground covered. I must believe, at some point in every person's life, they have observed or experienced some measure of leadership. I served in many SEAL commands and most performed the function of leadership well.

In the military there are leadership layers, much like most of you, but not all, would experience in your professions. In the SEAL platoon there are the worker bees, the lower enlisted mafia, generally E-1 to E-5. Then there is the Leading Petty Officer (LPO) who keeps the mafia on task. He is the first in line to solve problems that cannot otherwise be solved by the mafia. Then comes the Chief Petty Officer (CPO) and he keeps all enlisted members in check and on task, including the LPO. And of course, there are the two assigned junior officers, one with platoon experience and one who needs this experience. The chief is generally the most experienced and so the officers lean on the Chief for advice and consultation, but not exclusively.

Then there is the entire command structure and it continues to grow from there until we reach the Chief of Naval Operations (CNO). You get the idea, very much like any other disciplined organization. However, unlike civilian leadership, the military places leadership development and training on hyper-speed.

When you have your first child you realize how seemingly unprepared you might be for the moment. You have this newborn child and plenty was written, plenty enough was discussed, and much was investigated in preparation for this newborn experience. You've prepared the room in the assigned gender colors and worried yourself regarding all the necessary decorations. And, not so suddenly, the event is upon you and there you are enduring the sleepless baby and the diaper drama along with suitable bowel movements (clearly a subject we were never remotely interested in before the event). And of course the baby monitor listening for every conceivable noise, teething, crawling, first-steps, potty training, pediatricians, etcetera. So much more it would nearly require and entirely different book. But you do it!

Then comes the second and third child and you are comfortable enough in your experience. By the time the fourth child arrives he or she is lucky enough to get a pacifier, and the monitor becomes a mere signaling device. Similarly, experiencing leadership is progressive; however, those experiences shaping the model for most every individual in pursuit of this virtue can be accelerated. In the military one can find themselves with quintuplets in a matter of moments; and so, the military must make every attempt to find and develop its leaders quickly.

Wherever one might be during the call to step-up and lead; foremost, and perhaps quite exclusively, it is our affection for the object we are charged to care for while pursuing some objective. In other words, wise leadership is the coach who takes an affectionate interest in each member, in the team as a whole, while actively participating in the process and purpose of achieving victory or success to be shared by all. Compare this to any profession where the person in-charge has no interest in the people helping to achieve his or her objectives or success. There is no "buy-in" or compelling interest; there is no affection for those involved and even if success is achieved, there is no community or camaraderie of spirit to be shared with victory.

A person with wise leadership characteristics and one who practices such maintains affection for the ones he or she leads. They have a very actual, emotional intelligence regarding their purpose and they first see their purpose as supportive to the team. They possess a sense of personal obligation towards the people they are assigned, whether this is given by circumstance or by position. They clearly see both their roles as supportive and authoritative. We see this same role as a good parent; though we are the "parent" we are also the mechanism by which our children accomplish the process of growth and maturity. A comprehensive supporting role and a myriad of sacrifices will achieve this end.

The difference is, professional leadership roles do not nurture feelings; they nurture achievement. Perhaps the worst concept to plague our society, thus our lives, is "everyone needs a trophy". I do not wish to spend a great deal of time on this poorly conceived idea, but what it ultimately encourages is a collaborative effort based on the group's social and emotional well being. When this group's efforts produce failed results the reaction is to coddle them. Alternatively, a failure for goal oriented achievers is a call-to-arms as they prepare themselves to succeed the next time. My point here is simple: wise leaders have expectations regarding performance and realize positive emotions are produced through accomplishment and achievement, not the other way around.

When I volunteered for the military to be a SEAL and achieved this objective, the emotions and pride in my accomplishment, along with the few intrepid souls who stood beside me, were given to each of us by success, not through mere participation. These emotions cannot be artificially produced. This applies to ANY goal and achievement. If you wanted to lose 50 pounds and accomplished your goal, you would have an emotional experience as you dropped every pound. You would sense your achievement and feel the pride as you built momentum. And, that pride is an emotion better experienced through the exclusive wisdom of success as it requires no external or artificial influence.

Currently, the finest examples of leadership failure is the fallout from virtually any recent national election. Aside from the pathetic display of rioting and general anarchy, there was the safe space, coloring books, psychiatry, and companion pets to help stabilize emotions. Could we possible embarrass ourselves any further, wow! I simply can't imagine if SEALs followed up failure with coloring books and a box of crayons while Marines caressed rabbits in a safe space. We should be appalled regarding this absence of leadership, and much of it, but not all, is generated from the unproven theories of educators. Reality never has to trump or compete with theory; they're never in the same game, especially when it comes to real, authentic leadership.

Summary Points:

- True leaders balance a collection of values to nurture achievement by the group.

- Positive feelings come from achievement of a successful outcome by the team.

- Leaders manage the expectations of the group and coach each member to reach the group's defined outcome together.

- Good leaders lead whether that leadership role is assigned or assumed by circumstances.

Chapter 2
Titles Don't Make Leaders

Have you ever met the person who is always reminding you of his or her leadership position? When someone must remind others they are the leader this person is not the leader, but rather the person-in-charge. Assumingly with their position comes the expectation of respect. A person with real leadership characteristics compels others to follow because they appear and do as all others do in the group. Leaders have the same expectations of themselves as they have of others.

If in the SEAL Team we had members who did not assimilate into the rigors of physical training then, regardless of their position, they would lose momentum as an identifiable leader, no question about such. The Team guy's reputation is everything. If everything is there then others will be compelled to follow such a person. He does not have to be the fastest runner, the best swimmer, or the strongest individual; he just needs to be there to perform. This is but one aspect of the operator's life and it is pretty much the same in the world of specialized operators, be it Marines, Navy, Army or Air Force.

Leaders may have titles but titles do not make leaders. We often assume a title is necessary for leadership and we nearly expect leaders to have them. I've never saluted an unknown officer because I first respected them, I saluted them because it's a professional courtesy; it is a military greeting. I certainly respect the institution granting them their rank, but this does not extend to their person. And, I have saluted plenty of officers because their reputation came with respect. Rank is a title and though it may possess authority, it does not determine respect.

During some point in my career, I have experienced a small number of individuals senior to me, both officer and enlisted, that I wouldn't follow around a writing desk. Then there is a far greater number I would run through the gates of hell for because I respected them as men and as leaders. When one is a leader he or she does not determine if they are good, the ones who follow will determine the respect you should be given regarding your role as the leader. Roles are activities, sometimes exercised poorly and at other times demonstrated wisely. If you are a wise leader then you should know this: the noble ones who follow you determine the measure of respect you've earned.

If you find yourself in a leadership role then understand your title is assigned and your respect is earned. The goal of course is to lead others so they associate your title with the respect you've earned by the wise deeds you perform regarding the mission made up of people. And, those people, having accomplished their goals, will continue their gains towards further respect for themselves. This is the consummate "win, win" for all.

This has nothing to do with being accepted or liked as a leader. It happens naturally without artificial influence. You're better off never trying to induce acceptance; if you do, then you will have created an artificial follower. To earn the respect of followers in the real world they need an opportunity to lead and accomplish and achieve real things. Noble followers have the desire and interest to form their reputation as followers and earn their own respect as well. If you lead wisely then you become the model and mentor for those who will draw upon your example for their future leadership ability.

You've probably noticed I use the term "wise leader" as wisdom associated with common sense, knowledge, and experience. Certainly there must be more to this. If there is a common phrase associated with me it is this: "do the right thing." If your interest is earning respect from those around you, then do what's right based on values driven by a professional morality.

The group dynamic among the military's elite has no give for relativism nonsense. As individuals, they may have some personal issues, but the expectation of the group's achievements, success, and reputation are never marginalized. The point is this: if you "do the right thing" then you will pass along to those who follow your experience and knowledge. Doing so will imprint your leadership characteristics onto others just as they were imprinted on you.

Nature has a brilliant example in elephants where the matriarch leads a herd of elephants. The current matriarch learned from her female companions, more specifically from the oldest, most experienced and knowledgeable female. The purpose of this knowledge transfer is to avoid danger and follow years of imprinted routes to food and water. What's the lesson here for you as a leader? The role models you select for leadership must have the welfare of the herd at heart, and the herd is everyone up and down the chain-of-command. For the further purpose of this material I will use the title "leader" and you mentally place "wise" in front of such.

Not all in the hierarchy are leaders; therefore, the goal is to select from those who inspire professionally imprinted characteristics common to the herd. When you engage in an effort to earn respect, then it comes down to the selected leaders of your choice. If you choose poorly, then blame yourself and make no excuses. Excuses are never a suitable apology for a bad choice. I'm certain some behavioral scientist somewhere is losing his or her mental marbles right now.

Should your choice of role model be poor the solution is pretty damn simple, breakaway and search for the ethical individual. Look for someone in a leadership position demonstrating the professional expectations other noble followers have admired. And frankly, they're not as rare as some would believe. If it is suggested you work for a person who is a poor example of leadership then you must find, or wait, to imprint another. If you get this wrong then you will ultimately get the poor reputation that goes along with it. A solid reputation is only earned by the respect you've captured from the ethical wisdom you followed in the past.

I have been fortunate, as an adult and during my professional experiences to have been allowed to associate and follow solid leaders. They were never difficult to find. They stand out among and alongside their peers. Each of them had a different approach or personality to their leadership, but they had a professional morality and a direction for themselves and for me. Most, but not every decision made, delivered the desired results. It's fair to say when outcomes resulting from the decisions made are undesirable, criticizing a solid leader or a noble follower is a complete waste of time. Their self-respect and pride in "doing the right thing" is superbly more powerful than admonition.

Let me illustrate that point.

There is no room for missing your target in a Close Quarter Combat (CQB) scenario. During a training event I managed to miss my target not once but twice, the same damn target on two different runs! Every round missed in this environment is a liability and to say it is frowned upon is significantly understated, especially at the command I was currently assigned. I finished the day's runs with no additional mistakes but things like this linger in the mind of an operator. And, they lingered in the mind of the Team Chief as well… So he paid me a visit. Standing in my cage prepping gear and reflecting on my day's performance, and feeling poorly about it, his comments came with disappointment. He was right of course, and I should mention he was a very good leader by all measure. Finally it became my turn; I had no excuses for him but reminded him, his remarks were second to my own criticisms and disappointments in myself. Though it was his job and authority to have this little chat, he realized there is nothing to be said that would make me feel any worse for my errors. He understood, highly performing individuals like himself, are much harder on themselves than any words can offer; he left my cage understanding no further words needed to be exchanged. He was an intuitive leader and needed to do his job; I was an intuitive follower and needed to hit my target.

Summary Points:

- Leaders may have titles, but titles do not make leaders.

- You don't need a title to be a leader.

- Leaders keep the good of the group up and down the chain of command in mind.

- Find and follow wise leaders to use as role models.

- What you learn, model, and act on from those leadership role models you choose will ultimately determine your reputation as a leader.

- Noble leaders understand that noble followers respond best to guidance, not criticism.

Chapter 3
Management is a Position, Leadership is a Personality

Managers are useful; they hold the compass and point the direction others should travel. Leaders are essential; they hold the compass, point the direction, and step-off in the direction while encouraging others to travel with them. If managers and leaders were the same thing, we wouldn't use different words to describe them. This is not a condemnation of managers; they have their place and that place is necessary.

Having completed Basic Underwater Demolition/SEAL training I was assigned to UDT-11. Upon arriving on the Quarterdeck and checking into the command, we received our instructions and, having completed our supply issue, we assembled in the team room for an introduction by the Command Master Chief. Master Chief Hershel Davis was an imposing figure for sure. As a newly assigned member of UDT-11 just about anything seemed ominous and mildly intimidating, but the Master Chief was precisely what one would expect as an example of a SEAL. Actually, and at that moment, it seemed as though he was the entire community. As a veteran of the Vietnam War, with plenty of ribbons displayed and a neat handlebar mustache further accented by prolific eyebrows, his appearance was an attention getting characteristic. His command of speech and instruction were so well articulated, along with the excellent application of profanity, I was instantly convinced I was where I needed to be.

The Master Chief spoke of deployments as "Blue Chips"; essentially, we needed to deploy overseas as frequently as our human bodies would permit. This earned "Blue Chips" along with our conduct and our performance as a platoon member. Essentially, it is what one did that made them a Frogman, not the Trident on one's chest. Prove it and earn it, got it! I vividly remember this moment as though it were yesterday. He embodied the personality of leadership.

We spend a significant amount of time categorizing managers and styles. We use terms like micro, participative, coaching, authoritative, etcetera... You get the idea. There seem to be dozens of them and many of them are a bit squeamish for my taste. We see management as a position and refer to their styles like tools. We see leadership as a quality and refer to it as a personality. A tool is something you reach into the box for, you grasp the implement to manipulate some object; or, in this case a person or persons. What style is necessary right now in and effort to influence a person(s) and get the results I need? Management is behaviorally adaptive for the purpose of influencing outcomes. Is it fair to say, good managers attempt to derive a connection through positive well, constructed styles. This is the conscious choice to strategize influence. When properly exercised, it is necessary and persuasive; though, it is different than the personality of leadership. I could replace the word management above with leadership and it might sound equally as convincing.

If anyone had ever described the Master Chief as "management" I would have been completely lost as to who they might be speaking of. It wouldn't be possible to associate that personality with management. Did he manage things? Absolutely, but with a personality that was intrinsically influential and persuasive. His ability to manage was an intuitively expressed characteristic of his personality.

Leaders motivate and encourage the collective will because they possess, have experienced, and have learned enough to develop the necessary, natural leadership instincts required for their role. When they adapt to circumstance they're engaged in a naturally developed trait; it is an expression of their personality. Simply put, they may be exercising a style but it belonged to them anyway. A solid leader inspires others through the personality they possess. No one I know of in the military wants to follow the manager; they want to follow the leader. We are naturally drawn to leaders; we respond to the expression and convictions of who they are, and most often by what their personality has driven them to accomplish. It would be very difficult for the Marines to have assaulted Iwo Jima by following the managers. I doubt any good leader participating in this monumental undertaking gave thought to their management style; I seriously doubt they saw themselves this way.

We do not usually expect managers to exercise courage, selflessness, and sacrifice. They get a title for position; we will not necessarily give them the title of leader unless demonstrated. Should you exercise the above listed virtues, then you function as a leader, regardless of your title. These are characteristics of your person, not a behavioral adaptation for style.

We often blend management and leadership; we muddle them together as if they are the same thing, though there certainly is a relationship. In the SEAL Teams each department has a supporting role. The role is generally represented by members of the platoon otherwise known as Department Reps such as air, ordnance, intelligence, communication, and more. They manage the departmental aspects related to the platoon's success. And, among them are the up and coming leaders. The chief and the officers orchestrate this symphony of departmental managers. When it is run by a good leader, the personality and characteristics of the leader will become the personality of the platoon. When it is merely managed by an individual(s), this platoon has not the personality for success; it is static.

Personality is the life-blood of the command and the platoon, and it is natural for leaders to set the personality. Management alone can never develop the characteristics we associate with camaraderie and morale. Smart managers allow themselves and their people to be inducted into the personality of smart leaders. When one meets a leading person in an office, command, or company however, this may occur. Hopefully you are inspired by a personality; if not, then you met the manager. However, there are people referred to as managers; and, if you are inspired by their virtues as a person, then you met the leader.

In our world of relationships, not much works differently. Every meaningful relationship role you were commonly attracted too is attributed to a personality. Your friends, your spouse, your children, boyfriend, girlfriend, co-worker, teammate, neighbors, associates… and many, many more; this is the pattern for finding the leader. This is also the pattern for them, knowingly or unknowingly, finding us. It might be personal, or then again, professional, but this is why we respond to a leader. Military, corporation, and institutions of all types can be quite large. The leaders might not ever have met us, but we have knowingly connected with someone that may have unknowingly connected with us. I never experienced this sensibility with someone who managed me. I can give the names of most all leaders who made a difference in my life. I write "most all" because some were strangers but, in brief experience, I knew they were leaders.

Summary Points:

- Management is a style or tool. Leadership is a personality.

- Managers manage. Leaders inspire those they lead.

- In addition to the management role of giving direction and pointing the way, leaders travel with the group and point the way forward.

- No one wants to follow the manager. They all want to follow the leader.

Chapter 4
The Right Thing

As a parent, one or both of you is going to take a little time and teach your kid to ride a bike, without training wheels or assistance of course. You will discuss the essential skills necessary to ride the bike. When you're finished talking, and hopefully motivating them, then you pull a bike out of the shed and offer up a demonstration. Now your child will see how to ride the bike. We must wait until our children get on the bike and ride before he or she understands how to ride a bike.

We all pretty much begin in the same place, depending on our ability to grasp and apply concepts. However, educating a child in the equally important concept of gravity during their riding experience is generally left to experience. We tell them they might fall down a time or two, but it hardly gets mentioned. I might suggest we're teaching them on how to avoid it, but nevertheless gravity will eventually have its instructional moment and the child, or parent, cannot avoid this lesson. It's a fundamental law we rarely ever find necessary to discuss because it explains itself in detail when we hit the pavement. It's so damn unavoidable we actually place our children in some level of armor to prepare them for the upcoming lesson, nowadays anyway. The value of the lesson is so much more important than riding the bike, but because we are so certain of gravity's existence we leave the education to the finest of instructors, experience.

We understand this is an unavoidable law; it's universal, and one's choice to believe in it or not has no relevance regarding its existence or natural purpose. Once we have learned to ride a bike each of us gets to decide when and where we want to transport ourselves on the bike. We get to decide the speed with which we desire to reach our destination. We might decide on a less hazardous route; or, perhaps more challenging. We don't decide what is "gravity" – that's not up to us. We are permitted only to ride the bike and manage the bike so gravity isn't given an opportunity to harm us. The principal centeredness of moral law is like gravity.

There is much to be said in regards to doing "The Right Thing." I believe in moral gravity, even deranged minds do not get to decide on the existence of moral law, and we regard them as deeply disturbed because of moral law. Most all of us experience a sensation when a disruption occurs in a moral principle. As a young child, my older brother commonly took advantage of cookie distribution and ended up with the lion's share. I didn't need a Power Point to understand a feeling, and I was likely unable to give you the correct word to describe his offense. I do know this, what I sensed was a sincere measure of foul play and my emotions expressed a sensation. We sense the product of an injustice; it isn't strange we know at a young age when a principle, such as honesty, has been violated. We use the word "cheated" as simple language to assuage ourselves and bring attention to the violation, and not much changes as our lives progress.

Leaders know morality is like gravity in that it exist and there isn't much one can do to make it not exist. Leaders also know that just like gravity, trustworthiness, courage, honor, faithfulness, integrity, honesty, etcetera, are all law. Our minds can manipulate our choices, and these choices will shape our values, but we cannot manipulate moral law. A wise leader understands the necessary alignment of one's values and moral principle. A leader understands he or she cannot ever truly manipulate the gravity of moral principle. Morals would have no antonyms if they did not have a place in the universe as civilized, decent, and expected conduct… straight to hell with moral relativism.

An emotional experience doesn't require philosophy to split its hair, or any moral relativist to marginalize the principle. When we are lied to. When our spouse is unfaithful. When we standup while others display cowardice. When some are physically abused. When others are bullied to the point of fear. We are emotionally tied to all of these experiences. We lock our doors at night, protect our identity from theft, and closely observe our children at play because we all know the emotional price we must pay if we fail. We know there are those who will violate the laws of moral conduct. They do not share our values governed by moral principle; they purposefully avoid their restraint. And, even if one raises a child to perform badly, and removes their conscience for the principles of moral obligation, it does not change one damn thing regarding this gravity's existence. The emotional harm given and received by any moral violation is all the evidence one needs to understand the consequences of the transgression and the reality it creates.

I hope my point is made; I will labor no longer, you got it. The idea that doing "The Right Thing" is complicated is misleading. The idea that it can be difficult is equally as misleading. No! We do not always do "The Right Thing"; it is virtually impossible unless of course we are God himself. As a person, it is the insistence of your effort to ride the bike of decency; it should be your intention to stay on the bike of noble conduct, but even while giving it your best you will fall. Leaders make mistakes no question about it, but when they do it becomes emotionally assigned to them. They have fallen with an understanding, and have further learned the consequence of choice.

The experience of riding the bike improves each time we ride it. We tend to fall less and less as time and experience passes, but gravity is always there. Leaders learn from the fall more than from riding the bike; most good people do. Not all leadership decisions are moral, but certainly all decisions have some measure of consequence. One must begin with a foundation, and moral law is the cornerstone of one's leadership. Leaders know and learn they must align the foundation of moral law with their values; otherwise, they will continually fall and never transport themselves towards real leadership.

The Chiefs Mess is a body of all senior most enlisted members of a command; they are E-7 thru E-9 and possess a great deal of influence, which they have surely earned. I had a decision to make regarding a Senior Chief. The year before I arrived he was chosen by the Chief's Mess to be "number one" among all Senior Chiefs at the command. The title of "number one" is significant for promotion and places one at the top for consideration to be a Master Chief. The Chief's Mess was ignored and the senior most officers of the command choose another. Having come up through the ranks I knew this was against the grain of the senior enlisted… bad move.

The following year I was the Training Officer, and Tia (an abbreviation of his name), a friend for many years, now worked for me. He is the Senior Chief mentioned above and he possessed every meaningful leadership quality any person could ask of or expect. The Chief's Mess selected him number one again during the year I was his supervisor, but the Commanding and Executive Officer had another in mind (I should mention they were not the same Commanding and Executive Officer of the year before). I will say both were good men and good leaders. The other Senior Chief they wanted was involved in successful rescue operations of some civilians on a remote island. The Senior Chief involved was a corpsman and an essential member of the operation; these civilians had injuries in need of tending, the choice of this Senior Chief was obvious and sensible.

Both men worked for me and I was asked for a recommendation as to which should be given the "number one" title. Frankly, Tia did more and sacrificed more; he deployed frequently from his family and his overall contribution to the Team was superior. His conduct as an operator and as a person was exemplary; he deserved the title. To get passed over for this title twice would nearly be a nail in his promotional coffin. A single event such as the described operation above should not have precedent over a year's worth of commitment and effort. The Chief's Mess was correct for a second time but, not to disagree or battle with the Commanding Officer or his Executive, I chose the Senior Chief Corpsman; who was a fine man himself but I had the pleasure of both men under my supervision and Tia was clearly number one.

Against my own experience, against my doubt and intuition, against men of my equal leadership ability, I choose poorly and knew it when the recommendation left my desk. I was nagged by conscience. Shortly thereafter I was the one placing the call to inform Tia of my support for the CO and XO while he was once again deployed somewhere… I forget. But, what I will never forget is the broken voice and emotion of Tia from the other side. His voice conveyed so much more than disappointment, knowing this may very well devastate his future; to include, the additional income for his family because he was both a fabulous husband and father. He deserved it more than anyone I knew and I failed him.

Looking back, it would have been best for me to stand and fight the good fight for "The Right Thing," but I allowed myself the pavement instead. This was never to happen again. This occurred nearly twenty years ago, but I cannot shake it; it is emotionally assigned to me. Many of you have choices from your past and you cannot shake them away. This is because they're emotionally assigned to you. This is how good people and wise leaders know the evidence surrounding "The Right Thing" is indisputable; this is how we understand the consequence of moral gravity regarding the choices we make and the lives we live.

Summary Points:

- Just like the law of gravity, no one can change the laws of basic morality.

- You know you've bumped up against a moral law when you can feel that it has been violated.

- Doing the right thing is NOT complicated, despite what relativist popular opinion might have you believe.

- Leaders understand the effects of moral law and the positive or negative consequence, even when nobody is looking.

- The insistence of effort to do the known "Right Thing" because of moral gravity is the cornerstone of one's leadership.

- When you're given a lesson in this area, you will emotionally own it for the rest of your life.

Chapter 5
The Undivided House

You can let yourself be overcome by the people you lead; it might be that some never fully commit to getting on board. Be cognizant of the time they will consume and your responsibility to the others you're charged to care for. We have all heard the phrase "A house divided cannot stand." However, there's a professional circumstance, whereupon, if you don't divide the house it will not stand.

He said to me, "Never just take the Frogmen that are 4.0 sailors, take on the troubled few. A man who does everything you ask of him will never develop your leadership. The troubled few will challenge you and make you a better leader," the words of Master Chief Davis, paraphrased. The rating for performance has changed, but in the day a 4.0 sailor was the best mark one could receive. Reasonable to surround oneself with the best performers, this makes leadership simple. The underlying instruction was to have a small modicum of the Viking personality; the ones who train hard, but often play harder. Those few who might reluctantly comply because they're occupationally where they should be, but not very keen on all the rules when mentally and physically away from where they should probably not have gone. In case of war, we want to break the glass and release them to sail about on their longboat and settle the score; they're very handy. With appropriate leadership controls this is a personality we can salvage and use. SEALs are a cross section of society, they are hybrid performers, but they are people as well. Some people might not approve of the above mentioned few in fine dining establishments, but very much appreciate their rambunctious abilities when they need to strap their gear on.

Then there is the rare member who rows so vigorously away from professional discipline and responsibility they choose no salvation. I speculate this might be more common in regular military ranks, but in Special Operations they've done much to bear the title and wear the insignia. They've achieved so much, but for some, their behavior motivates them to cast it away. If I were a behavioral scientist I might have a shot at explaining this, but even if I could, what difference would this make. We cannot afford to prepare for those risky and worse case scenarios alongside the risky, worse case personality. We help each other for sure, but unlike today's emotionally focused overreach, we cannot labor over the individual(s) with the most problems as a priority. It is not that we shouldn't spend time helping others; it's very necessary, but when this measure of time becomes largely and exclusively devoted to an individual not willing or given to change, then it is also this measure of time subtracted from those willing to perform. Despite any leader's best efforts, these few will continue to break the professional and cultural ethos affecting the team, the command, and its ultimate purpose.

While in school, when your well-mannered child is made to sit near the incorrigible child as a display of how the little imp should behave… the longer your child sits there the more they are strained by the influence. We must assume there is some common transfer of influence. Would it not make sense your impressionable child is, in some way, being sacrificed for the betterment of this poorly behaved child? The disturbance interferes with the learning you want your child to receive; therefore, the time you've spent ensuring your child is mannered, behaved, and educated is somewhat eroded. Then a measure of your time is given to correct, as opposed to further, your child's conduct and performance. Essentially, as the parent, you've also become the extended parent for the problem child because you're picking up the responsibilities of the poor parent. Does not the time spent forging a behavioral path for the bad child result in subtracting from the good child? Ultimately, all involved in the correction have consumed time; time we could have otherwise used for the betterment of the good child. Sometimes a well-intentioned leader can find his or her house in turmoil. Mixed between the performers and a member with significant behavioral issues, allowing this co-habitation disrupts good order and discipline within the house. If this disruption goes unchecked, the ultimate purpose of your mission erodes. In this case, you must divide the house.

Leaders have an obligation to help others, but they have no obligation to sacrifice the community of people who want to personally and professionally perform better. This is not to say we turn our backs on the randomly misdirected souls who demonstrate an earnest will to improve or give them a hand up by providing a positive influence. I am speaking of the few individuals who, regardless of any constructive assistance, will deliberately meet your leadership efforts with an equal measure of resistance. You cannot help someone who willingly demonstrates his or her unwillingness for help. It is the same for family, friends, or a member of your team. You will travel further for family and friends, but in a leadership role you must weigh the consequences of allowing them to live in the house. When they're not responsive; when their activity is detrimental to the collaborative purpose; when their poor conduct and behavior is repetitive; when you're devoting more time to solving them as a problem and less time with the problem solvers, you've gone too far. You must be willing to let go. Some might see this as selfish, but I don't think so. The leader of those persons marginalized by the misguided compulsion to correct the consistently bad performer is selfish enough.

When I was first assigned to UDT-11 I became a friend to a charismatic and operationally minded fellow. Out of respect for his family I will name him Brian. Brian and I developed a very close friendship, though we were opposites in many ways; he was single and a heavy drinker and I was married and spent time at home. We were away from home often enough and I saw no reason to pursue activities compounding that end. I liked that he was well read and we enjoyed discussing a variety of topics. Like most Team guys, we loved the outdoors and spent much of our off-duty time engaged in these activities. He was far more gregarious than I, and had a compelling charm. He was humorous and clever; he also had a million dollar smile; I can see it right now. However, all the characteristics I just described to you vanished whenever he began to drink. The more he drank, the darker he would become. He became strangely paranoid and, the more he drank, the faster it moved.

He spent a great deal of time involved in troublesome moments. He was all of about 5' 9" and weighed in at 160 pounds… maybe.

He saw others as mischievous and conspiratorial when he drank, and generally picked fights with people much tougher than he; he generally didn't fare well in these encounters. He would just hit people without provocation; therefore, I did not spend much time with him during his after-hours excursions. It was insensible and saved me from getting wrapped up in his self-inflicted dramas. In the military we would refer to someone like him as a "liberty risk." Years passed and we remained good friends, but I was acutely aware of the strain and the limitations of our friendship. We both received orders to Red Cell. Shortly after we arrived I made First Class Petty Officer and, somehow, became the Leading Petty Officer (LPO) of the command. The Team guys already present, and equivalent of my rank, had significantly more experience and ability than I, but they were departing the command within a short period of time and so it fell to me.

I had no significant problem with my role, but to say it was challenging at times would be grossly understated. By this time, Brian was married but had no children. I was now single again, but just a few short days away from meeting my wife of 29 years. (However did she do it?) I was a friend in charge of a friend. My only conscious issue was I knew one of my leading troubled souls was going to be Brian. Another challenging aspect of this was the others knew how close we were as friends; of course, they carefully scrutinized my leadership, as it should be. I knew enough to do my job, but still felt compelled to help my friend, because I was his friend. When one leaves the house undivided, he or she begins to scold the smaller transgressions; this is a concession. It's as if you're reserving your energy for the larger ones you know they're coming and you're just trying to keep the house undivided. Don't do this. In short, Brian didn't exactly contribute to making my job any easier... and then came wisdom.

Friendship can sometimes be likened to banking. You both place money into the same account, but your friend makes too many withdrawals and the account eventually gets low. Following such comes the word "loyalty," this generally means they have little to contribute but would like to draw upon some of yours. He was a friend and a subordinate, but my house needed dividing.

Brian was becoming less a friend as he continued to pile on. The more deserving members needed leadership and it became an unfair distribution of time. There is a breaking point, some might call it enlightenment, but the time came and it wasn't pleasant. In a bar, Brian pulled a knife on a Team member, who was nearly a third larger and a boxer; surprisingly, this member just let it pass, for the moment anyway. Some time went by and one day these two decided to go have a drink together, whereby, Brian in his typical drinking modus operandi decided to assault this member again and struck him... really bad decision. Let's save some writing time.

I arrived at the hospital and inquired with the nursing station as to the location of my friend Brian. She said he was an ass; actually, more impolite words were used, but she did suggest I should take a look into hell if I wanted to find him... I liked her style. She discharged him because of his violent conduct... great! Apparently, he was walking the corridors. Before my Search and Rescue mission began I needed to use the facilities, and there in the restroom was a poor soul; other than his torso, arms and legs,

I observed this nearly human figure pondering his image in the mirror. I sympathized a bit until he looked to me and said the word "Rob," I really did not recognize him whatsoever. It startled me such that I pissed on myself… Damn!

Apparently, and as confessed, this Team member beat him beyond unconsciousness. I could literally count the individual hairs on his head; he had no measure of equilibrium as his head uncontrollably danced back and forth upon his neck. It was actually too large for his neck. He was so amazingly disfigured, and his eyes were so swollen I have no idea how he recognized me; let's all pay tribute to good bathroom lighting. I ran back to the nursing station and stated he could not possibly be discharged… he must have really pissed her off. She wouldn't admit him for gold bullion. I drove him home and stayed with him for the night as his wife was away, filled out Leave Papers for him in the morning and ran it up the Chain-of –Command for a two-week healing vacation. I checked on him every day, but it didn't improve much after two weeks. He turned a peculiar shade of green amid the bruising, so I had to run another Leave Chit for an additional two weeks. The Executive Officer asked me why Brian didn't run his own Leave Chit and I explained he asked me to do it for him, as it was a very difficult personal matter, but nothing alarming… the XO knew something was up but didn't pursue it. I was trying to look after both of them; this was a serious military matter and heads would roll. Actually, anyone could have rolled Brian's head - it was quite round. Team guys have a bout now and then, but this was over the top, not good!

And, the drumbeat of Brian's incidents continued thereafter, from missing movement to absent without leave, at times we could not find him... let's agree to etcetera. The time came for Captain's Mast, basically a disciplinary function in the military. He asked if I would be a character reference; I said yes, but that I would tell the truth and it will not be a favorable reference. Our time together began to expire after this, there were plenty of good times, but there were just to many withdrawals over the years. There was going to be a career for me regarding the many others who deserved more, and if I stayed this course I might continue with many more undivided houses. Many of us had done our very best for Brian, but it just wasn't meant to be; we were not psychologists. The consumption of time we all devoted to remedying Brian's behavior was of significant amount. He and I rarely communicated after Red Cell; he found God and had himself a bible study group. While receiving professional help he met and remarried a lovely gal and a beautiful person; things change when time passes. From his first marriage he had a son, and two smaller children from his new wife... they were young when in March of 2010 he put a gun in his mouth. He finished by stealing their time as well; it angered me. I suppose I'm as angry with myself as I was tired of the "one more time." I was in West Africa when my wife reached out to me because Brian's wife tried to find me for help, but there was no convenient way to contribute to his salvation until I returned. And frankly, I didn't think he had the nerve, this wasn't his first time. Wish I had done more; wish I wasn't wrong. Wish I were knowingly wise enough at the time to divide my house and safely place him where he could find a remedy for the things he battled within. The truth is, you do no one any favors by hanging on to disruptive behavior; you're not helping the troubled soul; you're not helping the people you lead; and you do nothing for yourself. Equally as important, you become a contributing member for the erosion of your mission; hence, that of your company or your command. The senior members who rely on you to perform your leadership task are unwilling contributors, until they step in of course. But then, the problem they need to repair first begins with you. Hope wisdom finds you sooner than it did me. When the time comes, divide the house, because you just might save all.

Summary Points:

- You can't prioritize the needs of the "problem child" over those of the team or the mission.

- A disturbing influence cannot be allowed to distract or create negative consequences for the team.

- You don't do anyone any favors when you cover for consistent bad behavior by any team member.

Chapter 6
The Personal Touch

As a leader you will find yourself balancing the personalities you manage; two people are never the same. With differing personality types and social beginnings you may need to address some issues. The most important aspect is this: if you are the first leader in line, solve the problem, and it doesn't always require regulatory processes.

Unlike the consistently disruptive personality, there are a number of individuals who are superb performers, but occasionally find themselves wayward. They're worthy of our leadership for sure. There are good people who do the wrong thing now and then, and there are bad people who do the right thing now and again. The military is the best youth program in America. There was a time when the judge said something to this effect, "pay the fine, go to jail, or join the military." I know a small number of Frogmen that received this ultimatum; they joined the military. To their credit they became great operators and excellent Teammates. Not to say they didn't find a moment or two of colorful activity, but they worked very hard and matured in life and profession. And, as a figure of speech, there were a few, very few, who never really made it past the surf zone. What better mentor for the newly assigned member than a leader who knows from his "experience acquired knowledge" the direction and guidance others might need. Again, SEALs come from every walk of life and you get every social composite the communities of America have produced.

In times past we felt more commonly equipped, regardless of our social beginnings, to deal with people of differing personality characteristics. Now, much of the culture today uses technology as a primary way to interact with others. In many ways it is essential, but when you're the leader, and the person you need to speak with is available, using technology as a replacement for looking them in the eye is unthinkable. If you're not keen on person-to-person communication, or, an occasional bit of confrontation to solve personnel issues, then may I suggest undertaker as an occupation. We need to manage relations, and we need to perform such in person as frequently as is possible in today's world. It will never be the way it was, but it certainly doesn't have to be the way it seems to be exclusively going either. Leaders are responsible for people; hence relations, if it is easier for someone to deal with the personalities they're charged to care for by not looking into their eyes then this person should be staffed with anime. We know more about one another than we ever thought or perhaps wanted; but yet, we have distanced ourselves from personally solving difficult circumstance of another's personality "in" person.

The military holds people accountable for their actions. We hold each other professionally accountable and, as a rule, we hold our members personally responsible. I hardly remember being seriously offended by a petty infringement from another. When larger personal matters surfaced between others, and it did, it sorted itself out in one way or another. We didn't have social media as a form of resolution, and we didn't have Human Resource (HR) officers adjudicating matters. We had ourselves and our mentors involved in the art of interpersonal communication. We now have a litany of offense, every thought conceived, each word spoken, deed performed, and emotion revealed. It's insanely ridiculous; too many in society are perpetually offended by the petty. Should our skin get any thinner we will be looking at one another's internal organs. By manufacturing and encouraging petty grievance the authentic problems requiring attention become misplaced. Let's give to those who are perpetually offended a "Sad Cloud" trophy and be done with it; only then can we focus on those who might sincerely need our help. The leadership guidance I received was this, "Handle problems at the lowest level." If you don't know how to solve the problem, then the problem is not yours to solve, seek counsel and guidance. The "lowest level" concept above is commonly learned in the military. You will never know the leadership capacity of your people if every time there exists a personnel issue it must be passed along or given to a well regulated impersonal process. But in an effort to solve these problems directly, and preferably in person, leaders need leaders to remove the chaff. This is never to ignore real problems, but every effort needs to be made to separate the genuine from the perpetually disingenuous and petty. Frogmen do this well; we have very little time for the offended, petty personality types... see a problem, fix the problem and generally this is done in person at the operational level for certain.

As the individuals given to petty complaint and ultra-sensitive feelings grow ever larger, the list of redress for supposed offense and that of the offended grows ever larger. From this, leaders, managers, and other company personnel become unnecessarily occupied by the Sad Cloud people; and now, we further concern ourselves with micro-aggression. This is the Sad Cloud people on Sad Cloud steroids. We continue to box ourselves into a required mediating department such as HR for hiring people, the hearing of complaints, and resolution of conflict. And not so strangely, HR has become the diplomatic core, replacing our eroding interpersonal skills and our once mediating competency with diplomat overture and social media resolutions. Diplomacy could be referred to as the art of delaying the inevitable... chances are; we're still going to war. Leaders must strike a balance and measure the need? Who is the personality? What might be the best solution? Can you resolve it? Will you need help? If someone your leading comes to you first, it's probably because they have faith in you. They need the personality of the leader and nothing else will do. If you prefer regulatory processes and mediation, then so be it! But like many SEALs, sometimes the box is a boundary we are not always willing to stay within. And yes! There is always an element of risk outside the box, but know your people and you will know your risk.

Striking the Balance

I had a fantastic Petty Officer who worked for me; he was stellar in everyway and definitely and up and coming leader. He frequently spoke affectionately of his family and I would listen to him and know he had good family values. One night he had a few drinks and got pulled over. In the morning he came to me and told me his mistake. He trusted me and exercised humility when describing his careless moment. Navy policy would have required me to bring this DUI to the attention of my superiors... I just couldn't do this. I asked if he turned over his military ID or just his driver's license, he said only his license. Civilians don't understand that in the military you are given double jeopardy involving civilian offenses. You are prosecuted and punished by the civilian authority, and following such you are punished by military authority. I asked him to give me time to think and I would speak to him later in the day. This incident would very much harm his career; I decided to be a senior man with a well-kept secret.

Later in the day we met and I told him my decision to refrain from sending it up the chain, but there had to be a consequence. He said he would accept any decision I made as payment. I had yet to decide what those consequences would be. I knew the civilian authority was going to get their payback, but how was I going to make this a worthy lesson for such a fine young man. I knew he felt badly, and that's a suitable emotion, but not payment for the deed. During the evening I pondered a suitable consequence and arrived at the answer. I knew how much he loved and valued family. He showed up in my office first thing in the morning and we had the closed-door meeting. He asked about the consequences and I told him he needed to search the public records for a local family, or the member of a local family, who was killed by someone driving under the influence. I needed to know about his findings first thing in the morning. He became visible upset, but I stayed on course.

The following day I asked him if he had the information, he replied he did and it was unpleasant. I followed up with, "You need to write a letter of apology to this family and I need to see the letter." Following such, I instructed him to "Omit your name and address, send it to the family and tell them you're sorry for what you've done, and what may have happen had you not been stopped." To say the least, he was shaken. He had the visual image of the missing family member and the sadness he would experience if it were his loved one. He needed to complete the emotional purchase before the real experience, and he needed buy-in before he bought it all.

With the letter complete he was given his last assignment. I told him to buy a dozen roses and drop them by the gravesite or the place where it occurred. He was worn, and sadly expressed he could not do this, it was heartbreaking and he became emotional. He contemplated doing it the military way, but I expressed he agreed to the consequences. At this point he expressed enough emotion I had to refrain. I told him to let me know when it was done; I have no empirical evidence he finished, but his emotions expressed a clear indication of his atonement. The payment had played its part, his emotions perfectly expressed his redemption and we both moved on. He did well; he's doing well, and has quite a beautiful family.

I could have done it the military way. I could have followed regulations, but regulations, as important as they can be, are purposefully removed from compassion. As a leader it very much helps to know your people, this way you can determine what measure of balance is required regarding your role as the leader of each personality assigned to you. This will be your opportunity to mentor and express some leadership versatility for the ones you lead. And though it is not for every circumstance, sometimes imagination in leadership is worth more than you probably ever thought.

Summary Points:

- Personally communicate with people as often as possible.

- Never get caught up in petty; it's time away from important.

- Know the people your charged to lead; this will help you solve many personnel issues.

- Always handle problems at the lowest level possible.

- Don't be afraid to use compassion in your leadership approach if it will better serve those you lead.

Chapter 7
Humbled Leader

Pridefulness and leadership never go well together. Don't get carried with how well you think you're doing. Just when you think you're on a roll, something seemingly small occurs, but it's really much bigger. I suggest you rely on these small events as indicators to proceed no further. When you have moments of self-adulation while in a leadership role, you will eventually say or do something regrettable because you think you just can't be wrong.

I found myself in this very situation with what seemed to me to be an inconsequential comment that affected some very fine young men. I said something to a young SEAL during a training evolution that was hurtful. I certainly didn't mean for it to be hurtful but, being confident in my critique, I carelessly phrased a question directed at him that was derogatory. I thought my comment would improve his ability to apply instruction... I cringe just writing this because I would prefer not to mention it at all. I really didn't give it a second thought after I vomited the words from my lips. But that's what happens when you're too damn busy imagining everything you say is important. I've had my foot in my mouth more than once, but as long as I don't develop a taste for it, or an appetite for that matter, I should be okay.

Upon returning to base and stowing equipment one of my young (and very stellar) cadre members came to me describing this young Frogman's disappointment. Apparently, this comment affected every young member of the platoon. I had no idea and began to ponder the comment. I didn't attempt to justify it, but I didn't think it serious enough to expect this reaction. This is what happens when you begin to believe everything you say is thought-provoking. It was very clear that the entire platoon was affected by my comment; nothing could have further substantiated my guilt. One person might be wrong, but they can't all be wrong. I asked the cadre member his thoughts and he found a polite way of saying it was harsh. He further said if I didn't want to make anything of it he understood. That's what subordinates say when they're telling you your comment was impressively stupid. He stood there waiting for my thoughts and decision.

As I replayed the reel of these words within my mind I saw myself as the young man I had spoken to and found I was quite disappointed. I said nothing for some time because I was still reluctant to admit my mistake. Then came the words from this young cadre member, "I have faith in you; you're always telling us to do the right thing." He patiently waited as if to say, "I can't leave because I'm waiting for you to show me how you're going to fix this." I told him to assemble every man present during the comment. Looking back, I'm glad this young cadre member came to visit because it's good when concerned others buy you a one-way ticket on the train of humility. Concerned others, if they have faith in you, know you're a better person and expect the best of you. When pride gets you there, only humility will get you out.

When he had assembled the troops I made a public apology to all, then I specifically spoke to the young man I had hurt and asked if he had some forgiveness, and of course he did. He was far more hurt because I had said it. I needed to restore his hope regarding his ability, but more importantly, I needed to restore his faith in me. He did great and performed very well, as did his entire platoon throughout the remaining part of this deployment… all very fine young men.

If anything will creep up on you, it's pride. Most people continuing to wallow in their self-importance end up with arrogance. When things are going well you're in a pretty good position to thank yourself; it's easy. When you're a person involved in a specialized program with special skills it gets even easier. When things are splendid, you will tip the jug of "I'm Amazing" and swallow a great big mouthful, and it can be so subtle you are unaware. This is when your mentors, friends, family, and even subordinates, as in my case, can help place you back where you belong if you will allow.

I have learned when you are the leader it is best to see yourself as the supporting element for those who work so diligently for you. With this in mind, you should know that good people make you good if you're a good leader. When you demonstrate your support for them, they will respond by returning an equal measure of their support for you. And, never questioning who makes the decisions regarding the role you play as the leader… they know this. What it demonstrates is your willingness to listen, inquire, and act upon their behalf if their suggestion benefits the team; hence, the overall mission, whatever this might be. Pride demonstrates superiority. If this is what they experience from you, then they might do their jobs, but they will never do their jobs better because of you. They have no compelling buy-in because it's all about you.

Since I'm on the subject, it's one thing to "misspeak" as though you were unclear... which was not the case with me. I hear this word used more frequently, and commonly by our national "leaders" and influential others. I generally hear the word "falsehood" as well. Anymore, these words more commonly follow up on the back of a lie, or a grossly inaccurate comment. They are purposefully used for cover; they are used as a replacement for an apology. It is doubletalk used to disguise their flagrantly intended misuse of words and truth. Their performance might deceive the unsuspecting few, but it displays arrogance and contempt for the people they lead. I would like to think the general audience of listeners sees straight through this veneer, but I'm not always sure. One thing is for sure; people who commonly repeat this activity are the marketing agents of pride and arrogance. So when you're the leader, and your moment for honesty arrives, please just say, "I'm sorry!"

I've had my share of run-ins with pride. I could have brushed those young men off; they would've done their jobs without question. What they wouldn't have done is forget the comment, and how it affected them. They would have never done their jobs better as long as my pride lingered. I have heard it said, "Never apologize when you're the leader;" apparently, it's a display of weakness. It is believed you will lose some measure of respect or perhaps, demonstrate vulnerability. Of course, you should never find reasons to apologize for the sake of an apology. But, when it is quite necessary to apologize and you choose not to do so, you only ever display weakness. You lose strength and respect, and when you sacrifice these characteristics you become even more vulnerable to pride. You will not be the leader, but will only remain "the person in charge." Where in normal life can anyone successfully display pride and arrogance in a relationship with others, whether it is friend, colleague, children, spouse, or parent and gain strength, respect, and security in these relationships? One thing I do know: if you regularly display pride and arrogance then people can never comfortably approach you. In this situation, the outcome for them is obvious, especially when you're the person in charge.

When your idea of leadership is that people exclusively support you then, for them, a mutual benefit doesn't exist. When their ideas cannot be heard over the top of your pride, they will not communicate. When you say or do things that embarrass people or cause them to unwillingly exercise humility because of your behavior, then you've become unapproachable and all indicators will tell them to "proceed no further." They will engage you as the person in charge only, but never as the leader.

One of my favorite military protocols is this: when officers and enlisted are dining in a common facility, and when mission requirements find it appropriate, the officers eat last. The people working for you have priority and take their portion before you step up to have yours. If there is but little left when you arrive to feed yourself, then so be it. Chances always are, if you look after them then they will divide their portion to ensure plenty remains to feed yourself; it's mutual. This is not done as a display of humility, but rather to demonstrate your effort to ensure they're cared for and to maintain their morale because you support them. Having written such, if you're always serving yourself first, then obviously you have a pretty high opinion of yourself. Those assigned to you will know you prefer the better part of everything for yourself and you are obviously not there for them at all.

Summary Points:

- Pridefulness and leadership do not mix.

- When pride gets you into a difficult situation, only humility will get you out.

- When you're the leader, and your moment for honesty about your mistake arrives, please just say, "I'm sorry!"

- Successful leaders see themselves in the support role for those they lead.

Chapter 8
Don't Lose Faith

When events begin to pile on it is easy to lose a little - or even a lot - of your faith. Please remember as the leader, the faith and hope of others might hinge upon your stamina to believe. Keep the faith!

He was a good fellow and came from an Irish-American family. When during his interview for the command he was asked how much he drank, he replied "plenty" as if it were an ancestral requirement. He commonly defended the Irish Republican Army (IRA) as if he had a few relatives across the pond that might still be actively involved. He was a solid Team guy you simply couldn't help but like. There was absolutely nothing pretentious about him and, in many ways, he was honest to an incredible fault. He was always good-spirited and friendly, and we enjoyed his genetically conditioned humor. He did his job well and was never found to be in trouble of any kind, at least not that I was aware of, and I was the Leading Petty Officer (LPO). He was the single most effectively functioning alcoholic I have ever met. He did everything well; he did his job well; he was exceptionally easy to get along with and he was funny. I don't remember a single complaint. And, he drank well… plenty well.

He had a particular coat he had manufactured from a field jacket that impressed me. He had sewn on a number of additional pockets into this coat in an effort to store beer. At the end of every workday he would have a case of beer, chilled and prepared for consumption. Upon completion of the day he would place them in his coat of many pockets and proceed to drink them until the pockets were empty and all was consumed. I asked him one day why he preferred his coat; apparently, he saw no reason to stop whatever he was doing to take a trip to the refrigerator, efficiently Irish I suppose. He had a Monte Carlo SS he was quite proud of and, to my knowledge, he stayed put at the command during most of his evenings and fiddled with his car. I never witnessed such, but I'm sure he made a trip from here to there in his vehicle during the afternoon or evening, but everything he wanted was about a block away. I don't remember him sleeping anywhere but the command. We were located in a private building and it was commercially rented for our purposes. Just 100 yards from our back gate was a bar, which didn't help matters, but Fran seemed pretty happy with just himself, his coat, and perhaps a friend now and again. We were located in Indian Head, Maryland at a small support base in a very small town.

Once I asked Fran if he thought he had a drinking problem, he looked at me as if I was inquiring about water, and responded as if I was concerned about dehydration. He basically stated, "There wasn't room for another pocket" as if he wasn't drinking enough… wise guy. It was as though I was communicating with the biblical character Jacob regarding his coat of many colors and asking if he could find space for purple. Then he proceeded to ask me questions about his work, being on time, never letting people down, all true no doubt. He was as good a petty officer as anyone would want or need. He just preferred to be left to his pleasant personality, and to spend his evening draped in his coat of many little beers. I liked him, but our roles were different and we had no previous history as friends.

On one very early morning a knock came at the door, it was Brian, quite drunk to inform me that Fran and he had had an argument at the base club. Fran was on his way back to the warehouse and lost control of his Monte Carlo SS. The roads were wet that night and Fran, along with another Team guy riding passenger, struck a telephone pole. Brian said I needed to come quickly. I dressed, I raced out of the house and ran down the street. It wasn't very hard to find the scene with the emergency vehicles and lights along with a power outage. As I approached I saw an ambulance was just departing. I introduced myself and asked the officer standing there the status of their condition. He said, the passenger was going to be fine except for a few scratches, but the driver would be dead before he reached the hospital. He further described Fran's body was seated properly facing forward but his head had completely turned itself around and was looking out the rear window. He asked if I would be willing to go to the morgue and identify Fran's body… and this I did. Following military procedures and a few days, we arrived at Fred's wake, paid our respects, and said our farewells. His Irish clan was every bit accustomed to a heavy dose of refreshments and humor; therefore, Fran came by his similar characteristics quite honestly. They all reminded me of him in a very pleasant way.

I became convinced of this one thing; too much freedom has a consequence. At Red Cell we had a limited measure of regimentation, which played out all too frequently, and sometimes poorly, for a military unit. The original members of this command seemed to have a better understanding of how to manage this difference, but for new members this was too relaxed and was unfamiliar to them. It is quite impossible to find balance when the scale your using has but one side to measure the weight. This was a problem for some. They had too much freedom regarding what would be a reasonable measure of good order and discipline; the weight of military regulation became the missing scale and unfortunate matters began to "pile on."

I had good officers but they, like me, were busy with the pile on and effectively trying to get the work done as well. Many unforeseeable events came to us as a surprise, and our command was very unpopular. Essentially, at Red Cell we embarrassed Commanding Officers of naval installations around the globe and this never makes for amiable relationships. We seemed to be constantly visited with retaliatory events by someone from somewhere. I was not privy to all the intricacies relating to many of these matters, but they seemed to be ever-present.

Faith in people is often like a watering can, when we have no faith the can is empty. When we have little faith there isn't much left; when we are losing our faith someone is pouring it out; and when we have an increase in supply it's because a few are helping to replace the loss. Fran's personal character was helpful in filling it back up now and again; and strangely, we were somewhat friendly, but never very close. I completely understand that no one gets out of living alive, but these things must be managed.

I find that many things contribute to a low morale, and if such a thing exists, we had the lion's share of nothing for sometime. Idle minds, idle work, loosely regulated standards, a barrage of accusations, a fusillade of investigations, and, when expectations are low, morale gets lower. It's then that some people, but not all people, will travel down the road of bitch and despair. Then comes the "piling on" of things other than business. Monotony kills the spirit and a need for its replacement often becomes the next problem.

The military absolutely understands you keep the troops busy; this is an imperative because boredom plays itself out in many, and often, unfortunate ways. Imagine Special Ops guys with little to do, a recipe for disaster amplified by the fact that our efforts were poorly received. Little appreciation was forthcoming; this most definitely will lead to some behavioral frustration. I am not applying this frustration to Fran, but this event took some of the wind out of my sail. No real operator anywhere wants the capstone of his life to be summed up by a few drinks, an argument, a telephone pole, and cold concrete slab for final viewing by some guy that was barely a friend.

Faith for me is empirical; it is a product of experience. It is not logic and it is not thought, but rather a sense. You can't display it in a jar, but interestingly enough you can show it to others and it is perceptible. It is equally as obvious when it is present, and perfectly obvious when it is not. All good leaders try to keep faith for as long as possible, because faith is intuitively linked to hope. People in the most difficult of circumstance have held onto to a hope for their survival; and those who pursue this virtue generally do better because it also gives them faith. I am certainly not making a comparison, and I would be embarrassed to imply my circumstance was remotely similar to many of these, but what I am stating is this: hope is the strength faith needs to prevail. One does not exist without the other. When faith is waning, we use hope. When hope is short, we apply faith. One is a strong belief (hope) while the other (faith) is a strong expectation… easy enough in my own mind anyway.

And so, it is necessary when things become progressively more difficult to have faith for those who need faith. I hope those I have led found some faith in me as I found faith in some of them. Captain Tarbox, LCDR Elson, and LCDR Irish, were good leaders. Tarbox and Elson were veterans of Vietnam, and brought with them their knowledge and experience. Irish had excellent leadership qualities from the get go, and as these three pursued a better structure for all… hope emerged. And though we continued to struggle now and again, they were responsible for improving the command, and led many of us to hinge our faith on their abilities. I would like to think these three hinged their faith on mine, and I believe they did.

The point is this: if any one of us displayed the possibility of "no faith" regarding the condition of our command, and the matters we struggled with, then we would be giving up on those who had little faith remaining. Imagine hope and faith as a hinge, they're two parts pinned together and have a beneficial relationship… it hangs the door. If one side or the other is removed you don't have a doorway any longer; you have an opening. And, then it does nothing to keep the cold air out, or the warm air in. People want leaders to do what is necessary to keep the door on, and keep the door working. Sometimes faith is the one thing you need to rely upon for the benefit of the people your charged to care for. Sometimes circumstance is hard to rise above, sometimes it might be impossible, but the memory of a leader being the last one to hold up the door is positively contagious.

Summary Points:

- Others are counting on your stamina to believe, always do your very best to keep the faith.

- When matters pile on refrain from displaying discouragement; it is time away from displaying faith.

- Faith is an expectation. Hope is the power behind faith. A good leader fosters both hope and faith in those they lead.

- Sometimes circumstances can be overwhelming, maintaining your faith and hope will keep your team together.

Chapter 9
12 Years of Strength Training

Perfectly Positioned

I have poor reflection on my childhood, as there seem to be many things I do not remember. I am always surprised when my brothers or sister share a story about us and I have little or no memory of it. Born in 1959 as Robert Martin, I grew up in the county of Los Angeles in a number of places. In my young childhood my father left; my mother was then a single woman with four small children. At some time during this period mother remarried. The road was rocky and intimidating because my stepfather was a former convict and an alcoholic. According to mom, he possessed an excellent sense of humor, but with his shaved head, prison developed muscles, and pronounced facial features, I didn't find him very funny. I feared him and gave him plenty of room, but unfortunately sometimes, not nearly enough.

Early in this strange little wonderland of life my stepfather would get physical with my mother and occasionally with us. My sister suffered more, my oldest brother perhaps second. My youngest brother and I were occasionally in the wrong space at the wrong time, but seemed to be of less interest. Circumstances do not always allow mothers to protect their children at all times, and some events which occurred, are better left unwritten. I suppose then, some turning of the head for togetherness and a measure of security might seem unnecessary to some, but at the time, may have seemed quite necessary to my mother... of this I'm sure. I did not have to display her courage, make her decisions, or fear to confront; therefore, it is best for me not to judge. Assuredly, she did her very best; life does not always give young mothers answers, but it's never short on plenty of circumstance; therefore, I must thank her. I will only say, keeping my distance was a valuable attribute that spared me some discomfort. Besides, I was the middleman with older brother, older sister, younger brother and myself. I was not the oldest, not the only girl, and not the youngest; therefore, certainly did not stand out.

Decision and Consequence

When you're a child you hardly know things are imperfect. Larger human creatures order you about and when you fail to follow instruction they make their point by any number of means because they can. We simply did as other children and assumed everything was similar... beauty of a child. I know this much, I was one angry young lad and would openly display my temper. I would physically display fury and fought frequently, these memories I do have. And, like any good and angry young fellow, I made myself busy in a few dust-ups. Apparently, there were a number of boys who were equally as pissed, so sometimes I won and many times I lost.

One very strong memory is a fight I intentionally picked with an older youth. He had significantly better instruction than I; he hit me so frequently and so precisely he winded himself at the expense of my face. This is the time when facial features become significantly disappointed with the decision of one's mind (and to think they're attached to the same apparatus... very disappointing). My temper was a problem and stayed as such for much of my childhood. A temper can make for some unnecessary agony; thus, the decision of my temper generally had negative consequence. When you're an angry young child you can hardly express or care about the reason why, you're just full of some unexplainable emotion.

The Mirror of My Temper

I saw my natural father a few times a year and, though I looked forward to his visit, an intuition was present that I was not a favorite. The good news is neither was my youngest brother; therefore, we had much in common as we were equally of less interest regarding his affection. My oldest brother and sister would occasionally be invited to stay with him; I envied them. On a few occasions, once to Catalina Island and once to his house in Oxnard, we all arrived for a few days. I remember being there but specific activities elude me.

I do remember a single time I was invited to stay with him and I was probably amazed while excited. We stopped at a gas station, back in the day attendants actually pumped your gas, and while the tank was being filled my father walked over and placed money into a cigarette machine. Back then you had to pull a lever for vending machines to dispense an item; he pulled, and pulled, and pulled again but nothing appeared. I guess he went to inquire with the attendant and then I pulled a lever and a box of cigarettes appeared. Unfortunately for me it was the wrong brand. With small pride I presented the cigarettes and he became very angry and scolded me. He just wouldn't let it go, and I spent the remaining part of our road trip as he indulged his temper upon me; I looked out the window and remained as such for the duration. In my mind I missed my opportunity to be a favorite.

And, as a child, I cannot recollect ever missing him again. He was the playboy type, fast cars, pretty women, and definitely single. I suppose having us around was an image killer; he was technically correct while being extraordinarily superficial.

A Sensible Alternative

My grandmother on mother's side was mildly short of the title "vagabond." If not for my mother giving her refuge in our home she may have had few places to rest. On those occasions when mother was about some errands grandma was the sitter. For reasons unbeknown to me, and more often than would be admitted, Grandmother occasionally would physically wear me down and wrestle me into the attic. I am uncertain as to whether I was just a common little bastard or she was just a mean, unhappy old woman; perhaps this combination of our two personalities simply collided. I found myself listening to her voice just beyond the door. I was a small child, but the memory of such has not been forgotten. Speaking of the boogeyman and of other such supernatural creature of doom... Ye ole bitch! The unfortunate wonders of cruel and unusual enforcement is that it just might backfire... God rest her soul of course.

A mild biography of grandmother would be that of an addictive gambler who never drove a car. She once owned a home but apparently grandfather gambled it away. They split over such; therefore, all the while with grandmother there was never a grandfather. He lived in the San Diego area but we did not visit him often, he was my favorite, so of course we weren't going to visit him much. She seemed to despise men...perhaps being male is how I got in the attic in the first place. Grandmother was a thief for sure; she worked at the Sheraton in Pasadena. And as a child, my impression of where dishes and silverware came from is quite different than most others. They came from grandma's pantyhose! Mother would pick her up from work and she would lift her dress and reveal a world of dining materials, large plates, small plates, bowls, cups, knives, forks and spoons, anything and everything associated with fine dining. Upon arriving home I can only suppose mother must have scolded her for her transgression just before she placed them in the cupboard (though I'm sure she rinsed them first). Thanks Sheraton! We ate on your china for years.

On those first experiences of my fear and what appeared to be the creeping shadows of my doom paralyzed me. I simply wouldn't move, only wanting to be one of the attic boxes. This sinister little kingdom became a rather useful place after a while; it went from spooky to divine refuge. Eventually, the more I frequented the place of my brief confinement, the more I began to investigate those attic materials without fear. My imagination of darkness was a lie; there was plenty of light from somewhere. And, the shadows of this temporary terror transformed itself into interesting artifacts to be investigated and a playground of sorts. The only witch, as I imagined her then, was just beyond the door and she would eventually leave. Perhaps she assumed I had fallen asleep. The luster for her design had failed.

I remember nothing about this house except the attic. Apparently, mother discovered her activities and quickly put a stop to such, now I would have to spend time with grandma... nuts! I have no idea how my mother collected this intelligence. When one is a child all that is known is the experience; I have no idea why my grandmother disliked me, maybe she disliked herself and it played itself out in unfortunate ways. In later years grandma and I got along fine. However, if you're reading this from heaven grandma you should know your effort didn't work. I thank you for the "strength training" contribution.

Best Bad Idea

For reasons I cannot explain, my stepfather took me to a bus depot where I was sent to a Catholic summer camp. I believe it was for three weeks; I was young and had absolutely no idea why I was there. My grandmother on my father's side was an angel and a matriarch of kindness. Each year she saved enough money to take us to Disneyland, cousins and all. That must have been difficult on a waitress's salary; apparently, she was determined. She was also the one who paid for my departure but with good intention, of this I am positive. I hear stories of the wonderful summer camp experiences, but I hated every minute of my internment. A good share of my time was spent in punishment because I lashed out. There was never any build up of the great time I was going to have; no understanding of why I was sent alone; no preconditioning of any sort as I was given a bagged lunch for the ride, some equipment, and I was off on a bus ride with complete strangers.

I was somehow convinced I was never to return home and that I had done something very wrong. If I had done something wrong it probably wasn't far from the truth. My counselor had his hands full and, as I had no additional expense funds for participating in crafts and other such events, I was bored and envious. And, because of my temper and my behavior, I was sequestered at times from events as I was busily involved with the art and craft of seemingly perpetual punishment. I'm quite sure I earned such, but you cannot always reason the "why" as a child.

Grandmother sorted it all out the last few days of my experience and I visited the camp store and bought some treats. It was too late for anything other than this, as my trip was ending and I was only too glad. I never made a friend and before sleep each night we were told frightening stories of superstitious, evil creatures lurking in the woods; perhaps the same ones grandma spoke of… excellent strategy to keep kids from wandering outside the tent. I cannot recall a single feature of my counselor or of any other, but somehow I recollect he was dutifully patient, but was never short on consequence. All I could do was observe other young lads doing the things I wanted to do. I look back and wonder why no one figured this out… give this shitty little kid some direction and a little focus. My early experience was that good Catholics are very diligent regarding punishment. I returned home and didn't really discuss the experience much, I was just glad to be away from the art and craft of my self-inflicted wounds. However, I will say, I very much enjoyed the outdoors.

Years later my two daughters asked me to talk about my childhood. I really didn't have much to tell them as I didn't remember much of my youth. But I did tell them about Camp Junipero Serra and my many walks around very large trees to pay for my transgressions. I did learn the song, "When The Ants Go Marching In," as I sang it quite often while in the penalty box. On one Christmas day my daughters arranged a remarkable gift. They put up a canopy and made a sign "Camp Junipero Serra," within which they placed an amazing array of crafts and things for dad to do. They put what little money they had and purchased these items. I was deeply touched, and I still am, as they had decided to remedy the past. They figured out what others so long ago could not; the finest Christmas gift ever received for sure.

While growing up, for many years we were Roman Catholic. I participated in many of the things Catholics do. I went to catechism on Saturday, church on Sunday, said my Hail Mary, my Our Father, and went to confession and so forth. For a short period of time we were admitted to a Catholic school. I suppose we were troublesome and eventual asked to leave; we weren't there for too long. In my particular circumstance the arms of the nuns may have gotten a bit weary; I know my knuckles got a bit weary. From here we transitioned into the church of the Pentecostal, which is significantly different. A narrative of which is reserved for later. But with the Pentecostals there is significantly more church time. On Sunday it is three hours in the morning, two hours Sunday night; a few hours Wednesday evening, followed by a visit on Friday. I really enjoyed Wednesday because it was Royal Rangers, and the men that led us kept us busy doing outdoor activities. A short message of faith and outside we went for a variety of things to accomplish. And not so strangely, I never found myself in much trouble.

If time in church were a monetary investment I would be a millionaire. If the Catholic fathers and sisters knew my presence there was forced upon me, as it was, and consumed an inordinate amount of my valued playtime, then they would have me in the confessional booth within a few short moments. And, during this confession I would make things up, pleasing the ritual but never admit in my confessional role the despair and pretense that existed. I would display my religious game face so as not to reap the wrath of parent or priest. The unspoken, and most immediate proclamation during my confession would have been this, "I would prefer not to speak with you at all." There were bikes to ride, street ball to play, and the stealing of candy from the local mini-store. Plenty of other interesting matters at hand for sure! And, of course, I apologize to all good Catholics for the offense regarding this most honest admission. I don't remember the name of a single Father or nun; none printed themselves upon my memory, but I certainly wish the kinder ones had. No doubt, the discipline was necessary and for this I must be grateful.

Having left the Catholic Church we started going to Evangelical and migrated to the Pentecostal experience. Prior to my high school years this experience was even more time consuming. Yes, I agree, there were moments of certain spiritual benefit regarding all, however, my transformation was not seamless. It was not the church that changed my views given to me by my experiences, but rather a person to be written about later. The worst of my fears regarding the Pentecostal faith was every Sunday night. Having spent my Sunday morning hours consumed by long-winded spiritual dissertation far above my head and desire I was never free to watch the two most amazing shows on television every Sunday evening, "Mutual of Omaha's Wild Kingdom" and "Disney." They would come on just about the time we left for church. Who wouldn't want to watch Jim Fowler wrestled creatures trying to save his own life while Marlin Perkins continued a narrative with no game plan on how to save Jim's life. And, Disney was just imagination. I needed this and, for a brief weekly moment, this would have been a contributive element for coping.

When I was younger I needed to visually participate in the adventure; I needed to partake in the imagination. My Sunday afternoons were defined by an expectation for one of my sibling or a parent to fall ill, so that I could stay home and engage my "wish I could." This is the only time I know of where healthy families ruin the best of expectations... damn! And for this, I need no forgiveness as the experience of religious ritual conflicted with the tenet of my faith. However, and I am certain it was of the best intention. Few ever ask a quiet, introverted kid his opinion.

I read every Jacques Cousteau book available in the library because I knew where I needed to be, I just couldn't get there. This was a disappointment but, you know how it goes, if you say, "I prefer to stay home," then you must need more church... a throat cutting exclamation for sure. I needed someone to understand I found solace in these episodes; I loved these things, this would have done more for my spiritual morale than anything on earth... it just wasn't meant to be. And, I still remain certain God would agree with my findings. God would have understood, of this I feel sure. I suppose one could argue that going from structured Roman Catholic to Pentecostal was like entering a "wilder kingdom." Eventually, I learned to listen, but I also patiently waited for a time to render my faith in God as was comfortable. No doubt a measure of discipline was encouraged. And once again, I apologize to all good Pentecostal people for any offense regarding this most honest admission.

I must abbreviate these younger years and move on smartly. As I look back they were difficult times, but far more difficult for my mother; she was also angry and it showed itself enough. She was a waitress and made great sacrifice. She worked late nights and needed to see her children off to school in the morning. I have no idea when she slept; I have no idea where my stepfather was, or where he was supposed to be. As a kid, you somewhat see your life as very normal. My aunt was a stay at home mother and died at 33 of ovarian cancer. She was a favorite and a beautiful person, so of course she had to leave this earth. But before she passed, her husband, my uncle Walter, played Russian roulette and apparently won... he found the only bullet. My sentiment at the time was life would improve without him. He was a mean spirited drunk and treated my aunt quite poorly; she was better off without him. The only person who deserved congratulations was my aunt, though I was too young to think of it at the time.

My grandmother on my father's side was a cocktail waitress, and grandfather was a house painter. They finished raising my cousins as grandmother had promised my aunt Jackie before she passed; three boys who were less than grateful. Once they left grandmother's care many years ago I have never seen them since. And as described, my grandmother on my mother's side was a waitress and a prolific thief God Bless her. That's a very short version of events and activities during the first 12 years.

And yes, there were good times. We were involved in street ball and school sports as well as the other imaginative games such as army, cowboys and Indians, baseball cards, and boyhood destructive activities such as murdering the innocent creatures of God, setting things on fire, and lifting treats from the store... etcetera. But much of the good during those first years did not imprint themselves upon me, as I should now hope. Immediately following those years the experience was demonstrably different. How does the path to leadership come from this?

From the "Inside" - *The Choice To Blame Or Not*

I understand it's hard to imagine something one does not always experience; it's hard to believe anything one does not sense. I did not initially have enough faith in others, or myself, because it was missing. There are many who began with more difficult circumstance than I, and I would be ashamed to compare myself to them. What I do know is this, people who commonly use negative circumstance as an excuse for their failure, become addicted to the use of excuses. It's their "routine for allowances" permitting them to reach ever lower. The leaders that emerged in my life didn't tell me what I couldn't do, their demonstration showed me how to start with the little bit I may have had. Certainly they were occasionally interested in where I'd been, but this was never more important to them than where they thought I could go. They never transformed a reason for this or that into an excuse for me. When you fire a weapon, and it is a bad shot, there is nothing you can do to change that shot, it's gone. The only thing you can do is to make the following shots better… this is what leaders do for others.

In Summary

What you as a person do with the version of life you're given is entirely up to you. Blame your choices on anything, anyone, or any circumstance you want. Be the victim, or be the hero, because it's entirely up to you. Spend your time being offended or spend your time being positive and effective. Whine or praise, cry or laugh, blame the past or use it as the testimony of your strength and stamina. Each of us is given our proving ground and sometimes the ground you stand upon is not so pretty. The testament of your life is never about how you started; it is about how you finish. That is a choice, and it is unrelated to material things, but can only be associated with your character. If you make it a "beat down" then you will never leave the proving ground victorious. If you make it "strength training" then you will graduate from the proving ground prepared for the remaining challenges of your life.

Chapter 10
Collisions

The virtues of leadership can only be given to others if you have them yourself; unless you've learned to wisely lead yourself, you've nothing to give.

If ever in life there's a myriad of indescribable emotions, it is when you have lost something - or something has lost you - that is so precious and dear, you cannot imagine your life without it; and then when you find it - or it finds you - the experience transcends simple words. A loved and beautiful family dog that has wandered off, perhaps a parent who temporarily lost his or her young child in a store, or a playground, or some other place; one can hardly express the emotions assigned to this experience. For the parent it begins with a calm calling out of your child's name; the next call tends to be somewhat more emphatic, following such you move about the house, the playground, or the department store to locate your child but they're not there. As you continue to search without locating them, your heart races and your mind begins to imagine. Your imagination guides you along the path of desperation because you've heard the tragic stories. They can only be safe in your arms. It seems as though time is racing past you, but then panic makes every moment seem like an eternity. You become increasingly more frightened because each and every second is a multiplier of your anxiety. You've searched about the small and large space within your home; your vision canvases the entire playground; within the store even clothing racks become the sinister agents of disguise.

You desperately inquire amid a familiar or unfamiliar audience of others. They sense your desperation and fear. You begin to wonder has some other person, or perhaps some unfortunate event taken my child away. Others begin to help, and the longer it goes on the more frightened you become, and then suddenly, however it may occur; your child emerges.

When your child appears, all your emotions suddenly collide and give way to an embrace and a few tears because your concern instantaneously becomes relief and affection. The layer of your emotions is so sudden the speed of light would be challenged. Initially your relief falls like glitter, as though your emotions require a continuing visual authentication, and then it rushes in like falling rain; descends like a waterfall, and ends as a river in a very small moment… this is how I describe redemption.

I suppose I was about ten or eleven years old when my stepfather found faith in God. Jerry Christopher Robertson, given away by his mother to be raised by his grandparents (his mother did not think she could raise two children and so she held on to the youngest). As much as I know, his grandparents were farmers in Kings County, California, which is an agricultural community. He worked the fields with little emphasis placed on his education; eighth grade was as far as he had gotten. He never spoke much about his childhood to any of us; including my mother. He joined the navy on his 17th birthday and, judging by his performance, he was a disciplinary problem. I reviewed his record and it is filled with one disciplinary function after another. He spent a whopping 18 months in the navy and was transferred out; he joined in February of 1952 and was asked to leave in September of 1953. He was considered anti-social and paid a visit to the Naval Hospital Philadelphia; where he must have been evaluated and not so politely asked to leave. He described his time in the navy as troublesome; apparently, much of it was spent in the brig. He was assigned to the destroyer USS Lloyd Thomas DDE 764... a destroyer, what a perfectly suitable vessel for an anti-social.

He passed away on 17 November 2001 with many of his childhood and young adult memories left unshared. For a brief period he was married to a concert pianist and they had a daughter together; apparently, after they were married, his new bride read the music (pun intended) and they went their separate ways. His daughter caught up with him years later. At this point in his life he had a firm handle on his person and his Christian faith, and it was a good reunion for both. Occasionally, he spoke of his criminal life, when back in the day finance companies would keep cash drawers; I remember this well because I made car payments to Household Finance Company (HFC) on Fridays. The cash drawer was up front and I paid cash; they would open the drawer and there was always plenty of money exposed. I saw his logic... why rob a bank. And so, he would rob finance companies on Friday and then he would lay low until cash got low. He never revealed the name of his partner in crime. Unfortunately for him, there was an occasion whereupon his partner and his partner's girlfriend had a falling out. She retaliated by giving law enforcement the location of their next robbery and the police were pleased to greet them and lavish them with bracelets. Essentially he was developing a career in crime, but I cannot write more because I don't know much more. He expressed to my mother his working childhood was difficult and punishment for his transgressions was met with time in the cellar. Whereupon, he would experience fear because Frankenstein was the popular horror of the time and he was always expecting a visit from Frankenstein in the cellar. As he told my mother, the thing he was afraid of the most was the thing he grew up to become.

Upon meeting my mother he had a troublesome past to put it mildly. He had difficulty finding work; however, he was a hard worker. Something you learn to recognize in others when you start working yourself. Looking back, he wanted some normalcy and married a women with four small children, not realizing this can be quite a trial for a supposed anti-social personality. Most men would argue this is not normal; he assuredly earns credit here. He assigned us chores and, at the age of eight, I was busy on Saturday mornings mowing yards, plural because we moved about frequently. His work ethic was impressive, not that I admired it then as I was made to be an extension of this effort. His only military quality was his inspection of our assigned chores. I seemed to excel at passing these inspection. This is where I was a suitable performer and I received a modicum of praise. He found low paying work, but indeed he went to work. Food was not abundant, but it was there; though, the choices were limited. I suppose he drank away some of the money but not all.

He also managed to grace the household with occasional disruptions. One of the most amazing events I personally witnessed was my mother striking him with a cast iron frying pan. He was off his game a bit, thanks to some earlier refreshments, and she hit him across the top of his head, dropping him to his knees. The event was amazing because she was holding only half a pan; the other half was on the floor. Any person knowing the structure and weight of a cast iron pan knows that anyone can use these pans as a replacement for kettlebell training, and yet, there it was.

Obviously there were some metallurgy issues with mom's pan, but it did impress me. I thought she might have killed him by the evidence on the floor. Then of course, mom had to render first aid as he was bleeding and I was told to leave the kitchen. I couldn't possibly have counted bouts, but clearly mom took that round. On occasions mom would leave him; she would have us assemble our precious belongings, place us in the 1950s Bel Air, and we would depart only to turn around a short time later and come home… nuts!

Perhaps his greatest strength was his willingness to read; he loved reading and enjoyed Louis L'Amour, a writer of westerns… not all was lost behind bars. There were a small number of things he was adept at, one of those being water skills as he would commonly take us into the surf zone and teach us to body surf. He was an avid abalone diver and, for a short period, had a boat and tried to make a living selling these aquatic snails. Times were good when we ate abalone for dinner; I enjoyed it and had no idea I was dining at the king's table… it's damned expensive. He took my brothers and I out shooting once in a while (no real safety brief, just find something to shoot at). As a former convict he was not supposed to have guns, this must be why we traveled out to remote areas for a little target practice. Convicts and guns, it's like Snow White and dwarfs; they just belong together.

He landed a decent job with Pacific Fence Company as a salesman of all things, and I suppose he did fairly well. He stayed with the company for sometime and then branched out to begin his own fence company. He had installed a fence for Reverend Fred Jordan, a man who walked the walk establishing missions in Los Angeles and other places in the world to care for those impoverished and needy souls left on the streets. Fred never seemed to have the checkbook ready to pay my stepfather for one reason or another, which of course caused my stepfather to return again and again. Each time my stepfather returned Fred would tell him about salvation and the love of Jesus. Then one day Fred had the check prepared and spoke one last time to my stepfather. Upon departing from Fred's house, my stepfather was nearing a collision between his natural and God's supernatural world.

As my stepfather departed and traveled along the road he reflected on his life and contemplated this faith in God Fred discussed with him. When he had traveled a short distance further he pulled his truck over to the side of the road. Fred had told him upon departing his home, it did not matter where you were; all you need to do is pray and accept Christ into your life. Not knowing much about prayer, he decided to say a prayer asking for help and forgiveness while in his work truck alongside the road. As he explains such, "It was as if I suddenly felt the entire world had been lifted off my shoulders; the weight of all my previous life was gone in a moment... I felt relief because suddenly something somewhere loved me. It starts like glitter; rushes in like falling rain; descends like a waterfall, and ends as a river in a very small moment; the lost child had emerged."

He never looked back, and though my mind was initially filled with skepticism, over time, God proved me wrong. Suddenly he comes home and hugs each of us; I never remember an embrace such as this before his faith. Initially, I was uncomfortable with this attention; perhaps, I was being set up for the big fall... an accomplice of sorts in the robbery of my affection. I internalized so much I had doubts about most people, especially him. He behaved differently; his attitude was so strangely positive, as old friends came by for a visit and to have a drink as in the days past, he would explain to them his salvation and faith; they stopped coming around. He displayed affection and care, and I really didn't know him any longer as Chris. We all called him Chris. He was never a father before, but now, suddenly, he behaved like one. And, as he became a father - and without any suggestion by others - we intuitively began to call him "dad." This transition of name to title was so seamless, and strangely compelling, it was as though a decision had been collaborated upon without our consent; we agreed without ever agreeing at all to call him dad.

An uncommonly friendly and generous personality emerged; he was humorous; he possessed joy. Before anyone got up, he would rise and spend time studying his bible like a scholar; he wanted to know everything and share all that he learned, but he never became an uncompromising zealot. He found a balance in his faith as he spiritually matured, and knew more than most the pitfalls of our human existence. He asked for forgiveness from all and began to travel along the narrow path described by his newly found faith. He had a very sensible approach, and was never eaten up by religious ritual. He asked to be an elder or an usher but was denied because he was a smoker, when practiced, according to the church, this defiled the temple that God had given him and therefore it was not meant to be... Scribes and Pharisees abound. Apparently, they knew their ritual but not their scripture. Even a thief on a cross can ask forgiveness and be remembered in heaven by God. I did not forgive them; I would rather answer to God if he will allow... the better Christian will always be my dad; he was not dissuaded in the service of his faith.

As he became knowledgeable in his faith he held family bible study, which I enjoyed. Then he held a men's bible study; then he began to help as many others as he could in their life and faith. Eventually, he made it back into prison, but as a saved man; a man on a mission to help those who were now wasting away their lives as he once did. His business began to do better and his sons worked alongside him installing fence. We worked hard like many others in life, but somehow we simply didn't give a damn about how hard we worked. He was a different and wonderful personality to be with; a day with him was generally an enjoyable day indeed.

At first I was bewildered, and I struggled along for a few more years. I was still relatively quiet and still moderately troubled. My temper was still a problem at the age of thirteen; the future was obviously brighter, but I suppose my anger was all about the past. I was definitely introverted and in many ways a loner. If it were not for dad's patience, and somehow knowing where I was and how to get me where I needed to be, then I am uncertain as to how matters would have turned out in this life for me. He would talk to me about my temper; he would keep me near the faith; he would spend time with me and listen, and he would instruct, and teach, and advise, and demonstrate just as any leader would. How did the man I did not want to know become the man I wanted to be? We had no closeness before he found God, and I had no real affection towards him before God found Chris. I was quiet about most things, and as far as I could see then, before his salvation, he was just another larger human pissing me off. And now he is washed by grace, forgiven by God, and walks on some kind of water for a confused, troubled, adolescent soul he called son.

He told me to count to ten while I was getting angry, and at the end of ten, think about whether or not what I'm going to be angry about is worthy of my temper. It sounded too simple; and yet, each time I practiced this the further my temper would travel away from me. I realize now, much of my temper was directed at the ones closest to me; perhaps, I was tired of the middleman position and being a rather unexceptional human within the circle of my influences. I didn't need to worry about this, dad was an unexceptional person by every standard on earth, but he was led to find God, and God's Son led him to find the cross.

As time moved along dad developed the personality of a leader. Once, he was just the person in charge because he was the largest human figure in the room. Now he was the leader, demonstrating his exceptional ability given to him by grace. He was given a title by the virtues of the respect he earned because he understood the principles of moral gravity and the demands of his faith. I simply wanted to follow him because he displayed wisdom. And so, for him the wisdom was rather simple, "love the Lord your God with all of your heart, with all your soul, with all your mind, and with all your strength. This is the first commandment. And the second, like it, is this: You shall love your neighbor as yourself. There is no other commandment greater than these." Essentially, you cannot give something to a neighbor, a family, a friend, or to any other that you do not possess yourself. You can give nothing of yourself to another if it is not yours first to give. He found loving God must be observed if he was to love himself; now that he possessed such, it could be given to another… like me, like my mother, and my brothers and sister.

In Summary:

Intelligence might be the smartest thing in the room, but wisdom is always the most intelligent. And, like any wise leader, and like so many other virtues in life, you can only give leadership away to others if it belongs to you. The instrumental collision of events was finished. I observed, I contemplated, and I began to practice dad's instruction with plenty of mistakes for certain. How was I going to find myself out from under the clothing racks of life? How was I going to emerge? I had no damn idea.

Chapter 11
Leadership Starts From Within

To Pursue Any Noble Thing You Must Take The Leadership Role From Within

I never gave one thought to leading others, though, as time moved along I developed a better understanding of how to lead myself. In my high school years I was keen enough not to listen to everyone's opinion or follow the crowd. As a matter of point, I don't remember ever following the mainstream. I had a few good friends but never found interest in popularity. I had a few questions in my mind about God's role, and with these few questions I leaned on dad and also discovered C.S. Lewis. The first book I read of his was, "God in the Dock." Then I read more of his work such as, "Mere Christianity," "Screwtape Letters," "The Problem of Pain," "A Grief Observed" and other works. C.S. Lewis did more for my faith and understanding than any man on a pulpit. His logic reached me and, from the Word, dad's instruction, and C.S. Lewis, I found stability and started leading from within; essentially, I constructed the foundation for the house where leadership could live.

The Good Omens of Circumstance

When I was eighteen I lived in an RV storage area. It was owned by my dad and adjacent to our fencing company. I kept a Marlin .22 Long Rifle in my small trailer for just the occasion about to be described. Very early one morning there was a ruckus when just outside, and a distance away, I heard windows crashing and noise being made all about me. The camper I lived in was suitable for me, but very low end and of no interest or value to the discreet, RV thieving connoisseur. I collected my trusted Marlin, loaded of course, and then began my SEAL quality recon… perfectly unaware I was performing such at the time.

Upon exiting my trailer I observed a fellow much larger and somewhat older than me break a window to a camper and enter. I set up for him upon his exit and when he came out I leveled the rifle and aimed it directly at him. I gave him commands and he reluctantly responded, but I had the gun so arguments were not to be heard. About this time, I heard crashing at the other end of the storage area and never thought there might be two robbers. At gunpoint I escorted my captive down to the other end and had him call out his buddy while I stayed in the darkness. He must have tipped him off by calling out the wrong name because, as he descended the camper steps with a myriad of goods, he broke into a full gallop. As he ran, my attention broke from my captive, and I fired multiple times at the legs of my fleeing suspect; he got away… damn! But, as my captive saw an opportunity to flee himself, he was also met by gunfire… I missed him too, but he hit the ground anyways. I missed both of them and was very disappointed. My lesson from this was, it is best not to take firearms training from former convicts. I had no idea regarding the remaining ammunition in my trusty Marlin. I was surrounded by a fence topped with six strands of barbed wire. And, I clearly didn't understand the law regarding the shooting of fleeing unarmed intruders… perfect! I wasn't concerned in the least and strangely unafraid.

I had to communicate to someone what was going on, but I had this bigger guy to be careful of, so I escorted my captive into the office and placed a call to my dad. He told me to call the police and he would see me later in the morning. He must have had great confidence in me, because after his instruction he hung up the phone and never called back. After placing the call to the police, my captive informed me he was not going back to jail... interesting fact. He picked up a piece of angle iron my dad had left on a desk in the office; he raised it above his head and prepared to strike me. I lowered the rifle and shot him through the shinbone. It was a total hip shot. He crumbled and started screaming as blood emerged from the hole like a small, dribbling fountain. I was enthralled and wanted to see the damage so I told him to pull up his pant leg, as he continued to refuse my request I lowered the rifle and threatened to shoot him again should he not decide to accommodate. He had to take me seriously because I just shot him. Had I shot him again there may have been a few issues with the law, but at the time this was simply not relevant; I was certainly clueless regarding the law. When I saw the wound, it looked as though someone took a ¼ inch drill bit and drilled right through the center of his shinbone. Go figure... I aim the gun and I miss; I hip shoot and I hit center target... amazing. Fortunately, dad was short on medical supplies so I didn't have to pass bandages. He was bleeding a great deal for such a small wound; I just wanted to get him outside so he would stop bleeding all over dad's carpet. I didn't even know enough to tell him to apply pressure. I hadn't the mildest of sympathy for him. He just needed to be shot and that was that.

The police showed up at the gate and I emerged dragging this jackass while still carrying my Marlin… damn he was heavy. The cops drew their weapons and asked me to put my gun down, this made plenty of sense because the officers were completely unaware of how perfectly safe they were when I aimed my trusty Marlin. I let the officers in the gate and they proceeded to chalk the many rounds I had fired. A very kind officer took me aside and told me precisely what I was going to say. He coached me before the investigators arrived. He had me repeat it several times and told me to say nothing more. He had me recite it and then he went about his business, but would return now and again to remind me. Additionally, he explained to me how close I was to being arrested, and this being the reason why he was so adamant regarding my testimony. When asked by investigators, this is what I said and nothing more.

My captive gave up the name of his accomplice and the police drove straight to the accomplice's house and arrested him; of course he had a record, both had criminal records. I was told by the police the one I shot was a past felon, and it was a matter of time before he would once again emerge from prison to commit more crime. Apparently, the bad guys were unaware of the 18-year-old Marlin-toting-trailer-tramp who missed everything while aiming at moving target; however, he was one hell of a hip shooter. My dad arrived in the morning and asked why all the blood; I explained the events of my early morning pre SEAL adventure. He asked if I was okay, I said sure, and then he said, "Good! Clean up the blood." Apparently, it's hard to impress a former convict, even if he's a man of faith.

I went to court to testify and there he was. I never got a look at the one who successfully fled my gunfire. However, the one I shot had a cast covering the full length of his leg. Officers came along while I was waiting in the hall and thanked me, joked with me, and congratulated my criminal capturing success. The paper featured the story that afternoon; it described a Wyatt Earp gunfight between some kid and a couple of mean hombres… not even close. There was only one sloppy gunslinger amongst us. Many folks, especially elderly came by and brought baked goods and such because they were thankful. Dad enjoyed some pastries and, by the end of the day, said, "I'm proud of you son." I didn't know it at the time, but this was my preliminary moment, an unusually good omen of things yet to come.

As luck would have it, I didn't receive a higher education. I never remember college being a family discussion. Graduating high school in 1977, one could get by needing nothing more than a solid work ethic… I had plenty of this. The family business was fencing, it included residential, commercial, farms, tennis courts, backstops, and anything and everything related to keeping things in, or keeping things out. Cows needed to stay in and thieves needed to stay out. The work was as hard then as it is today. I was just a few years out of high school when my dad sent me to contractor's school for the company contractor's license. This I accomplished by taking in these few lessons from my contractor's education: you're never right; people are going to sue; most everyone will complain; and you will more than likely lose in a court of law… money well spent.

Being young and looking into my future I was not exactly inspired. I think all good men and women who work with their hands are noble indeed, but I did not want this for my life. I couldn't see any other future, as nothing inspired my attention and I was rather short on dreams. I became good at the fencing trade and seemingly thought the expectation was for me to eventually take charge of the family business. I needed more and, if it were not for my younger brother, I would never have become more. I would never have been a Navy SEAL. When he described to me this daring element of shadow warriors we both decided to have a look. Remember, the notoriety of SEALs today and their popularity did not exist in 1980. We visited a recruiter and we were quickly sold! Any person allowed to live and work by the sea, and eliminate (or, as the Master Chief would put it, "turn birthdays off") perfectly healthy humans for bad deeds done was a suitable life for certain. When inspiration arrives, expectations emerge.

My brother and I decided to join the navy together and both become SEALs. We ran together, swam at the YMCA together, and went to enlist together. During our physicals I was called first and completed the process, raising my right hand to defend the Constitution of the United States. Then came my brother a few hours behind me, where he was strangely diagnosed with asthma. He played high school sports and no such ailment troubled him. The lady that diagnosed him was nothing more than a middle aged institutionalized medic. She placed it in his record and refused to enlist him; we were both heart broken. As I was on delayed entry, we had time, so he put some money together and went to a pulmonary specialist. The doctor performed a complete workup and called the diagnoses complete nonsense. My brother followed up by taking these medical results to the navy. And, as any well-trained government institution, they refused to accept the results. He was given no second chance, and no second medical examination. What was recorded was recorded, and no discussion was to be entertained. The U.S. Navy couldn't possibly have made a mistake with a stethoscope.

Being a SEAL was my brother's dream first. Still to this day, we infrequently talk about it, but when we do, I can still sense a small measure of his regret regarding this dream. He had to live it vicariously through me; what a great Frogman he would have been. Today he owns a fence company, doing exactly what we were both doing, and nearly where we were doing it so many years ago. I am humbled by how well he accepted his version of life, and I will always feel as though I owe him something for delivering into my hands the version of the life I received through his inspiration and encouragement... forever my thank you.

Certain navy ratings applied to the occupation of being a SEAL such as Radioman, Quartermaster (as in ships navigation), Corpsman, Boatswains Mate, etcetera. I was convinced I was going to be a Quartermaster and took the Armed Services Vocational Aptitude Battery (ASVAB). This is how the military describes an examination, my math scores were so impressively low the recruiter told me I qualified to be a ships cook and nothing more... potentially, if I knew how to use a paintbrush, I could spend some time outside and help paint the ship gray. Then I suppose, the only good news was that I absolutely did know how to use a paintbrush and came from a very long line of skilled house painters. I could not be a SEAL with these scores; the recruiter was pushing me to sign the contract; whereupon, I inquired how long I must wait to retake the ASVAB again. He said 30 days; I said I would return in thirty days. The trouble I had with the navy's ASVAB math was that the majority were math word problems. I wasn't particularly fond of math so this didn't help whatsoever. I visited the local bookstore and purchased every word styled math book I could place my fingers on. Then, before work and after work, I studied those books like a scholar. Thirty days later I sat down for my next and final ASVAB… the results were spectacular. I was nearly offered whatever I wanted; and yes, I could become a Navy SEAL; and yes, following Boot Camp I went on to Quartermaster "A" School and did very well.

It was as if matters within me were hinged on my taking the lead in my own life. As I reflected on my most recent circumstantial moments I somehow knew that I was where I needed to be. I was comfortable in this design, and when I found inspiration I focused on my expectation. Expectations are like pieces of a mosaic. When they're properly placed where they belong, they will assemble a picture. When this principle is applied to our life we call it ambition, a path, or a dream. To pursue any noble thing you must take the leadership role from within. It is either because of, or regardless of, circumstance one leads themselves towards their preferred, or discovered design. My brother went on to own a company, and I went on to become a Frogman. Each of us used or replaced a circumstance with an ambition to succeed.

In Summary:

People who have good leadership characteristics find their way through the traffic of life's circumstance. Amid my many faults, I had somehow acquired one superbly useful characteristic... I was disciplined. Where this came from I have no idea, but it was exceptionally useful. And, when I discovered a path, I employed my expectations, and this developed a picture, and the picture developed a dream, and I disciplined myself to achieve this end because of, or regardless of circumstance. I know of no successful leader who expresses low expectations; or, is given to low levels of applied discipline to the specific objective(s) they pursue... onward to BUD/S class 120.

Chapter 12
The Wisdom of Following When Following Wisdom

There are followers who prefer only to follow and nothing more; this is best for them. Unfortunately, sometimes they go on to being in charge of someone, but have no discerning experience or desire for leadership. They were always meant to simply follow another. And then, there are followers who prefer to become leaders. They learn to lead themselves, and then choose to wisely follow the ones who will lead. If you are a discerning follower, then the leadership, or the lack there of, is available for observation. All of us choose to follow someone, something, or some path. And, the variety of choice can be plentiful, but the criteria is rather simple. Leaders present us with confidence not bravado, inspiration not arrogance, humility not pride, demonstrable competence not a discussion, selfless not selfish, disciplined but compassionate, and having faith or purpose in something greater than one's self. All of which leads us to the leadership professional.

Disciplined but Compassionate

The day following Boot Camp I got married to my first wife. We were very young and both came from working class families. The navy didn't pay a Seaman Apprentice (SA) much. We had an apartment in El Cajon, California just outside San Diego about a 30 minute drive to the command. I was not clever enough to realize the added difficulty and pressure I had placed on myself by having a young wife while going through BUD/S. Prior to BUD/S she followed me to Quartermaster "A" School in Orlando. I had to put in a Special Request Chit to have the Chain-of-Command approve me living with my wife. I was only an E2 and the navy wasn't keen on allowing such a junior member of their navy live off base with a spouse. I ran the request chit up to the Master Chief of the Command. He was very Southern and salty; I stood there while he asked a few simple questions. This inquisition has never left my memory.

"Did the navy issue you a wife?"

"No Master Chief!"

"Did you find one in your Sea Bag?"

"No Master Chief!"

"Do you know why?"

"No Master Chief!"

"My navy doesn't issue wives; that's why she wasn't in your sea bag."

"Yes Master Chief!"

This didn't seem to clear things up. It was as though I had failed to properly request her from supply. I was mildly confused as though I was supposed to bring her along as evidence. I stood there for some time as he continued to stare at me; I was quite aware we were not having a discussion. I was intimidated for certain and he looked perfectly angry. He softened after a brief period and expressed how difficult it would be for me, so young and married in the navy. "Chances are you will not be married for long." He approved the chit with visible concern. One does not become the Master Chief of a training command unless he or she has leadership characteristics. With this same measure of concern he asked me to leave his office.

I left feeling a bit like a common virus. But, amid the discussion in which I hardly participated, there was the glimpse of compassion, as though he had read the book and knew the story; or perhaps, had lived the experience. This approval was pleasant news to my young wife; she completely didn't understand the military's business of permission. When she asked about the approval process and I explained my brief conversation with the Master Chief, she was not significantly impressed with her status as shortly less than worthy of a sea bag. It is best when some things are left unsaid; communication is not always the heart of a good marriage.

Except for my bike, we had few possessions of any kind. I used my bike to transport myself to and from the command. It was bare bones and I struggled in the humidity of Florida to keep my uniforms dry before morning inspection following my ride to work. I added hours to my struggle, especially when I arrived at BUD/S. Though I was not short on determination, it would have been wiser to leave the girl at home. And what the leader knew and what concerned him came true; three years later she was gone. Other than the one occasion where she served me papers, I never saw or heard of her again; apparently I left little impression. She had found another while I was on my first deployment and that was the end. No worries, she was replaced by an authentically remarkable woman.

Humility not Pride

When I checked on board the Basic Underwater Demolition/ SEAL command the first person I met, after an exercise of intimidation on the Quarterdeck, was a Second Class Corpsman named Bob Scandiffio… may he rest in peace. He and I were the only two present for Class 120, and he suggested we go for a run down the beach in our new jungle boots to help break them in. We both quietly stomached the blisters forming on our feet because it wasn't manly to express pain while enduring an impressive measure of stupidity. He was a fantastic personality, an upbeat, positive individual who could motivate just about anyone. He never stopped talking and, since I wasn't much of a conversationalist, it worked out perfectly (other than the currently forming blisters). Unfortunately, I had also acquired shin splints while at "A" School in Orlando, Florida; the SEAL Motivator had me running at night in my boondockers on pavement to prepare me for BUD/S. A boondocker is a common boot in the navy, a massively produced piece of heavy black leather with a comparatively hard sole. I might as well have run with heavily tarred Brazilian nuts duct taped to the bottom of my feet… thank you!

The following day Bob asked me how my feet were and I told him not good. He replied with laughter, describing the very same condition of his own feet… we laughed at ourselves as he gave me something for the blisters. He certainly didn't have to give a damn, but he did. Bob was a Second Class Petty Officer who obviously outranked me but he never talked down to me; or made anyone that I know of feel less about themselves. He was quite assertive when necessary, and got things done. Any one of us could rely on Bob exclusively. He became our class LPO by default, as the original LPO quit and there were no standing First Class Petty Officers. How lucky was I to have met him the first day I checked into BUD/S. Prideful and Bob Scandiffio were antonyms to one another, an exceptional man indeed.

Confidence not Bravado

As our class began to form up, the numbers of which I do not remember, we were assigned our rooms. I was first given a room with a fellow named Larson, should my memory be kind, and a few others of course. He was as large a personality as he was of physical size. He had been in the military for 5 years and professed to have crossed over from the Marine Corps. He was never short on giving us his verbal resume, and by all appearance he looked to be the image of such. He was convincing and spoke with confidence and bravado. In my naiveté I initially developed a measure of dependency on his bravado for the things yet to come; besides, he was the senior man in the room so it seemed appropriate to listen… and listen we did. On many occasions he would discuss the necessary ability to succeed and our potential lack of ability to make the cut… perfectly theoretical.

I began to question his authenticity because his person was not so strangely missing the character of leadership. With some people there comes a point where you realize they are not talking to you, but rather they're using you to speak with and convince themself. This is when one's mouth is communicating in plain text, but transmitting Morse Code to one's mind in an effort to send a message right back to oneself. With this type, their resumes are continually offered along with a gross embellishment of a few truths. They use it like an exhibition where at first you think you see the painting but eventually discover it's facing the wall. He was gone within a day of Hell Week and I never saw him again. I had strangely placed a moment of confidence because I was duped by bravado. I had briefly followed a display, but it was never up to any other than me to make the choice of who to follow.

Demonstrable Competence not a Discussion

Within my class, of those who remained, there were good officers and solid enlisted performers. The beauty of BUD/S is the playing field is level; everyone gets the same rigorous treatment, and each challenge is endured by all who've come to fight for the title. And, it is quite fair to say the class leader endures a bit more, as the weight of the class and its performance rest upon his ability to lead. Lieutenant O'Connell will always remain my favorite SEAL officer. As a graduate of the U.S. Naval Academy and our class leader, he seemed tireless; perhaps the hardest working man I've ever met. Sometimes I think he worked to find more work. He was strict when required and he followed the rules, but not without compassion. He motivated us by demonstration, he had high expectation of himself, and this encouraged us to achieve the very same. He was the consummate professional. He possessed warmth when he laughed and a good sense of humor. I saw him as balanced, fair-minded, and a concerned individual for all. He seemed to have the ability to graft common sense into situation. He also never made an excuse for anything, and he was always accountable.

After BUD/S I served in his first platoon and, following such, I served under him in the SEAL Team FIVE Training Department. He took the time to become a friend, and we enjoyed discussions now and again. We understood our military relationship and I never thought to take advantage of it; I simply respected him as a person and a leader. I took pride in following his example, and never took offense to his instruction or reprimand. He was the person whose painting always faced the observer; you simply wanted to get nearer to have a closer look.

Inspirational not Arrogant

Ensign Wall was an inspiration to all; he was in BUD/S class 48 as an enlisted man during Vietnam. As he told it to me, he got out and went to college then sat on a rock for what became just short of a decade. Now married with children, he returned to the military, completed Officer's Candidate School and became an officer. Apparently, because of his separation from service and newly acquired commission, he was required to go through BUD/S a second time. I suppose he needed a waiver for his age. He would now attempt to complete BUD/S a second time with class 120 while being thirty something.

He possessed every motivational characteristic anyone could possibly ask of another. He was tough and commonly injected humor within a bit of misery. Nothing appeared to hurt him, but I must believe it did now and again. He did everything as well, if not better, than us younger fellows. He looked after each of us, especially more so when our herd began to thin. I have no idea how many times my mind said to itself, "If he can do it twice, then I can do it once," and I am quite positive that I was not the only one having this internal conversation. When he stood up for graduation the second time, his uniform was an impressive decoration of ribbons and medals. He had earned a trident as an enlisted man; then he earned another while an officer... that's damn impressive.

Sadly, I saw him only one other time during my career for his dive requalification when I was the Training Officer at SDV Team ONE. He was the same Hank Wall... nothing changed. In a very good way he was definitely eccentric; preferably out of the box, undaunted, and one of the most inspirational and motivated individuals I've met... with him present there was never any excuse for quitting. He had combat experience and achieved twice what we accomplished once.

Selfless not Selfish

Ensign Baugh was my boat crew leader and both a fine man and officer. There was never any doubt he was going to take care of us. When it came to the academic side of dive phase he helped plenty with the math. Clearly he was the smartest guy in the room, and potentially one of the smartest guys in the Teams. He was definitely a scientist, but a seriously selfless person who provided positive direction and leadership. During Hell Week he could not get under the boat; he must have been 6' 5" or taller and therefore he was not level with anyone assigned to the crew. Our crew was six foot or taller, but he was just too damn tall.

During the first few days too many guys had quit the crew and only five of us remained. It would be a few days before enough quit for us to inherit additional help by the reorganization of the boat crews. The only thing Baugh could do was to pull us along with the bowline, or push from the rear. I remember being pissed off at the guys who quit, as we would run along with just four under the boat. Because of such we lost at every event... we sucked and paid dearly. Without Baugh we would have had zero forward momentum. At this point, no one was interested in physics and Baugh wasn't preaching it. This is where reality of selflessness trumps science and theory. In another time and place Baugh would have developed some sort of fulcrum to aid our weary necks and legs; unfortunately, we were just oxen. To his credit he never gave up on the crew and never stopped pushing or pulling us along. He was not the most inspirational of fellows, but he was there for us; he was as weary as we were for sure, if not a bit more.

It would be unfair not to mention Ensign Hinckley (spelling), I believe he was the class Honor Man, but I had very little time with him until my second platoon. He was also a good leader and during our deployment he did an excellent job. He was keen to listen to the advice of the men serving under him, and quite often employed our ideas. He did not impact me like O'Connell or Wall, but he was steady for sure and I very much liked him as a person.

The Professional

I am certain that every BUD/S trainee has had the one instructor who left a lifetime of impression. For me there only one, Bob Donegan was this person; may he rest in peace. He was one of our First Phase instructors, and previously I had no specific image of what a SEAL was supposed to look like. Everything about him exuded professional. He was an enlisted man at the time, but retired a Lieutenant, and he exemplified SEAL. He looked to be made of granite; he articulated his direction; he demonstrated his physical expectations; he led training evolutions with precision; and he expected nothing less than quality because this was precisely the life he determined for himself.

On one occasion he was demonstrating how to tackle the high wall on the obstacle course when, looking up from below, it seemed very damn high. He suddenly lost his grip and fell to the ground with a thud. He hit the ground on his back and, without hesitation, he briskly stood up and informed us this was the improper technique. Then he proceeded to tell us how he was about to demonstrate the proper form and technique required to complete the obstacle. At this point I wasn't listening anymore, assuming, any moment, he would try to catch his breath or check for fractured limbs, something anyway… nope! Now, in my mind at least, he possessed the characteristics of superhuman. Many of us looked to one another as if to say, "Did you just see that." He completed the obstacle properly and descended with grace.

There was so much more to Donegan than the physical. He was inspiring and motivated the ones who chose to be better because he was the example. In a place like BUD/S one cannot have an expectation that all will succeed; quite frankly, the majority will fail. Donegan delivered his expectations with little visible sympathy for failure, which is precisely what was required. But I would never think to suggest he was compassionless, because this would simply be untrue. His effort to impart his knowledge and experience, along with exercising his described role as an instructor, helped to determine his leadership approach. I did not know him on a personal level, and our paths never crossed again. When I heard he had passed in December of 2016 I was extremely sad. His obituary read precisely as I would expect: married to his wife for 35 years, 8 children, 13 grandchildren, three Masters Degrees, an accomplished black belt, and so very much more. His manners, demeanor, and conduct always gave to me a sense he was a very noble and honorable man, and indeed he was. Is it so strange a man I met and observed 35 years ago on the grinder at BUD/S, and did not personally know, displayed the indelible characteristics I describe. The characteristics of wise leadership don't evolve, they have been the same since time immemorial.

These were my most notables; there were others, but these few made an impact prior to the Teams. I allowed myself to observe, make a choice, decide on who was going to be an influence, and then permit myself to be led by them… it was never their choice. As time passes so does being in charge, but real leaders become an indelible memory, a timeless imprint assigned to your life's experiences. We never really forget the contributions they bestow upon our person. So, choose to wisely follow and you will wisely lead.

Believing in Something Greater

When you earnestly search for something you may know generally what it looks like, or perhaps exactly what it looks like. When you follow someone it is much like a search, while searching you look for information or clues; when following you look for the clues regarding one's characteristics. Because leaders are people they're not perfect, but what sets them apart is their continuing effort to pursue, learn, and improve the virtues of leadership. Most importantly, they apply the science of leadership in the building of and the caring for the people they serve. They believe and understand the purpose for which they lead is a purpose that is greater than themselves. A wise parent serves a child so that they might grow to be loving, decent and kind; a wise teacher serves so another can be educated; a wise coach serves to give others the experience of achievement; and a wise military member serves for the safety of our nation and the maintaining of our freedom. There is the common thread of sincerity and trust regarding the characteristics of the follower and the leader... this is why the relationship works. Leaders see their role as a service; the same can be said of followers. If someone was to ever tell me, while being a parent, that my wife and I were not in a service role when raising our children... they would be grossly mistaken. And, what we most often find in our life is we are commonly involved in one role or the other, but more generally both.

Amid the few principled virtues described, and there are more, we need to be able to determine a person's leadership authenticity and also build our own. So we search, we find, we observe, we decide, we commit; and from such shape our leadership values. Starting with the discerning or wise values we decided we needed for ourselves; the discerning values we decided to find and follow, and the discerning values we decide to use and apply when in the leadership role. Followers and Leaders search for similarly decided upon attributes. This is why there are also bad leaders and very bad followers. If the values you search for are not noble virtues then you will follow the leadership values of the ignoble. It's a pretty simple life formula. Pick the right people and the right people will pick you.

This is so important because I see people, younger and older, being duped by titles, certificates, position, education, and a myriad of other false authenticators. I'm not suggesting people who have such are not leaders, but I am saying it is not a prerequisite for leadership authenticity according to the principle-centered ideas presented in this chapter. If you should ever wonder the difference between associated leadership and authentic leadership then just compare our politicians with our men and women in uniform. One is elected and the other volunteered. One has every available perk and the other has comparatively few. One seems to have, or suddenly acquire wealth, comfort, and influence, the other a fresh pair of boots, a rack, and a mission. One is willing to sacrifice little, but the other is willing to sacrifice it all up to, and including, his or her life. Now, I cannot say this about all our politicians because this would not be true. But what can be said is, when comparing these collective bodies relating to leadership authenticity, the military member takes the risk of self, for country, and to stand by their comrades in arms at the cost of life. Politics aside, their purpose is given to something greater than themselves.

Summary Points:

- As a discerning follower, YOU choose which leadership examples you will follow and allow to shape you as a future leader.

- True leadership is, ultimately, service to others.

- A leader demonstrates their leadership ability through their attitude and actions towards those they lead.

- Good leaders constantly improve their ability to lead by also observing the actions, habits, and attitudes of those they follow.

- Follow the right people and you'll become a better leader worth following.

Chapter 13
Breaking It Down

Leadership is timeless, regardless of where we are in our history; it seems to be a part of our human DNA. If we were to travel back in time, or advance forward to this current age of technology, it really wouldn't matter. We want leaders; and at some point in life most of us are given an opportunity to be one. Some people don't want it, some people don't know what to do with it; and some people accept it as their role because they understand its purpose. Your role as a spouse, parent, sibling, friend, mentor, teammate, manager, nurse, supervisor, or coach, etcetera gives you an opportunity to positively contribute and lead others. Sometimes it might seem to be in small ways, but not really. If you're willing and able, then the size of your leadership contribution should be measured by how well you led the people given to you to lead… it did for me. Looking back upon my road in the plainest sense it would read very much like this.

I picked a road to travel with the version of life I'd been given. As the road cleared a bit I chose the direction I needed to travel and followed the version I destined for myself. Along the way I found a road atlas to faith and began to understand there was something greater than myself. I wanted the road of authenticity; I led myself down this road while occasionally hitting a curb now and again. I turned right on the narrow street of principle; I turned right again on the narrow street of moral gravity. Along the way I passed through the gate of my mistakes, but I didn't leave it open. Eventually, I followed a solid stone path leading me up to the house of demonstrable leaders. When I took the initiative to knock on the door the personality of many leaders emerged. I observed the things they did while ensuring it was as they said. This helped me understand the remaining part of my travels, so now I knew the direction to go and how to lead others. The gate of mistakes is always there; however, just beyond it is the path of experience… so I kept learning from it, but remembered to close the gate behind me. I had the version of life I decided on, and now I could build a house for others and be there to open the door for them.

- *Everyone gets a version of life.*

- *Only you can decide on what to do with the version.*

- *Only you can decide on what to do with every available opportunity.*

- *Lead yourself to follow a principled purpose; make it noble.*

- *Lead yourself somewhere that inspires you; make this noble.*

- *Find the positively principled personality of wise leaders.*

- *Follow these leaders and you will gather the information for leading others.*

- *Lead with what you've learned, the knowledge you have, and the experience gained.*

- *Do the right thing for those willing souls you're charged to care for.*

- *Be there to inspire and influence the dreams of other who desire to be leaders.*

We don't always need to associate leadership with something grandiose. Each of us is responsible for those in our circle of influence; you know them. People reading this book will never know the many leaders that exist and positively contributed and influenced others with their role. It might just be the simple things; some might call it a drop in the bucket, but this is precisely what waterfalls are made of. I quite confidently know many leaders, and many of them are not SEALs, but just fabulous people.

You don't have to wear a Trident on your chest to be leader.

In some ways everyone has their platoon and you do your very best to take care of each member of the platoon. Just because you're in the leader's role doesn't mean the result of influencing another is going to be positive in terms of outcome. There are plenty of very good parents who could not otherwise lead an incorrigible son or daughter away from a negative direction. The problem is not with the parent; it is the one who chooses not to follow a better direction. Essentially, they have yet to lead themselves by the positive values given and demonstrated for them. Parents might wonder where or how they may have gone wrong… no need to go there. By and large, there is a point where each of us chooses the influences and the direction for much of our life.

The physical aspects related to being a SEAL or any other Special Operator are renowned. There is much more in the Teams and our military and we are fortunate to live within the land of many leaders. This is very unique. It is fair to say not everyone in the armed forces is a leader; this is true. However, the military presents one of the single greatest opportunities to become a leader; the road is there to follow if you choose wisely.

Not all, but many of my mentors were veterans of Vietnam. I made my mistakes along the way and I still do. The leaders of my generation gave me consequences, but not condemnation; so long as I wasn't perpetually repeating offenses. If they sensed my better intentions by my better demonstration, then all was well. And, I am sure they saw within us what looked to be them so many years ago. Not all, but many Team guys I know came from rugged beginnings. They were middle class or less, but they found their life stride… they found purpose in the military. A few did not, but they were definitely in the minority; they were covered by a very large shadow cast upon them by the leaders.

In much of today's civilian populace, anyone asked to leave for standards unbecoming would be the offended victim of insensitive conduct by the leaders. We don't see the point in the philosophy "Everyone gets a Trident." We only see everyone must earn it everyday, and that is the standard for the Special Operations community. That is the standard for great military branches like the Marine Corps. We don't mollycoddle people; therefore, the performance is better because we haven't covered the virtue of accomplishment with the blanket of make-me-feel-good.

Nothing I personally or professionally wanted just magically appeared. There are requirements and conditions that need to be present. They were available, but still needed to be pursued. It is like a vegetable garden… pick the fruit or let it spoil; it was entirely up to me. The measurement of effort applied to one's ability to lead is directly related to one's ability to wisely follow. Therefore, one's effort to wisely follow is the result of one's effort to wisely lead one's self.

Then, there must have been an element leading me up to this point. Unlike today, I had no real information about what I was getting into. Now, anyone from nearly anywhere can Google or Youtube aspects of BUD/S. I'm almost glad I didn't. If someone was to tell me they're going to tie your hands and feet together and toss you in the deep end of a pool I might have thought a little harder. Yep! You're going to spend a week without sleep; carry boats on your head; PT with a log; run miles in soft sand, and be as cold as you've ever been… Sounds great! Sign me up! The problem with being an introvert is you don't generally ask a lot of questions, but you do make plenty of observations. When I saw the quality of people about me and how decidedly unique and difficult it was, I was all in, and I stayed in. What intrinsically pursued principle was there? There must have been some available attribute besides just following an instinct, an instinct to a vision, and a vision to an expectation until I reached my final objective. But like so many others, what made this pursuit achievable? How about the equalizer of opportunity available to all, categorically know as self-discipline… I'll just use the word discipline.

Discipline is not restricted by circumstance. We all have access to it, but some of us choose to never use it. Many have made a better life for themselves by capitalizing on this attribute of discipline. It can be the greatest of equalizers if you decide to use it, but it does require a commitment. It is purely voluntary and shows no favorites. It produces nearly all of the attributes one would need to prevail in an effort to achieve an objective, whatever this might be. We see it as many things but summarize it with one word: discipline. We define it by using words like heart, intestinal fortitude, will power, motivation, and inner strength, etc. We also know it's strictly a mind thing; it relies on your decision to pursue it and then use it. We associate it with physical things like weight loss, overcoming addiction, or learning to play the piano. However, we rarely associate it with the things we cannot always see. Such as one's commitment in a relationship; or perhaps, a devotion to one's faith.

Even principled attributes like honor, courage, and loyalty require discipline. Discipline is so encompassing that if you adopt its strengths, then from it you can develop opportunity. Any wise leader I ever met was disciplined regarding the role they served. It doesn't necessarily mean they were disciplined in all categories of their life, but they were for the purpose upon which they were intended to lead. Fortunately for me, and with my shortcomings, I possessed bucket loads of discipline; this forged for me opportunities as it does most anyone who uses such. When we apply discipline toward a positive pursuit it can be transformational.

Whatever circumstances from the past or present exist, one can apply discipline to overcome much of it, if not all of it. Each of us is given a version of life, but you don't have to settle. A dedicated push towards discipline can lead you past the boundaries of your circumstance; it can produce amazing opportunity. Matters that disturbed me from my beginnings were used by discipline to make me better... I applaud their contribution. Only self-discipline could exploit this, and allow me to be a Navy SEAL and a leader... like so many others before me.

Chapter 14
Conclusion

I think we have plenty of leaders and, in some way, somewhere they're busy leading someone regarding something that needs to be done. We knowingly or unknowingly see them everyday; and though they seem quite ordinary, they're rather extraordinary. They contribute to the lives of one or many, but they're often too busy leading to notice their impact. They leave the business of demagoguery and the legacy chasing ideologues to clamber for their audience. I'm writing of natural leaders, natural as in sensible, and sensible as in wise. They look after community, neighbors, family, friends and strangers. They work farms, enforce law, heal the sick, educate children, run tech companies, and develop real estate. Some volunteer for our military, some are entrepreneurs, some are small business owners and most are exceptional family leaders. How do I know this... well, in one-way or another, I've met them all. They're grand without being grandiose; they enjoy the principles of positive influence for the common and virtuous good of most others. They have an intuition for boundaries; they know within the smallest or largest spaces of human influence and behavior they must maintain their focus to accomplish positive objectives. They see matters, small or large, they know must be attended to and they "lean in" to get it done!

They're busy dealing with realities, whether that is a disabled family member, community outreach, or a military unit. They understand the obvious good regarding the health of the team in an effort to accomplish the mission of the team no matter the size. And, they never attempt to artificially stimulate success by way of imagined achievement; or to spare feelings… it must be authentic. They do their very best to ensure their deeds replicate the words they've spoken. Not all, but most, possess within their character a measure of humility. Which means they have little interest in being recognized, but more commonly find an interest in solving real problems, positively influencing results, and positively shaping lives. And, not so strangely, because of their personality and performance, be it large or small, they get recognized regardless… I might even use the word discovered.

They're not perfect at everything, but perfectly ready to solve anything within the function of their leadership. For them, leading others is an imperfect science because, like themselves, the subjects involved are imperfect specimens, but they commonly have a willingness to move toward the best available outcomes for the willing.

The ones I have followed look something like this…

They are Patriots, believing in their nation as imperfect as their nation might be, for them, there remains no better place on earth. They believe in family and community, and like so many others they believe in a right and wrong. When a promise is made they do their very best to keep such. If they give someone their word and shake hands then it's a contract. They believe money doesn't make you rich, it just makes you comfortable. They've probably met plenty of the poorest rich people on God's earth. They believe in working hard and earning their keep wherever that might lead them. When someone wants help and it's within his or her ability, they'll help. They have a humbleness regarding their purpose and existence; they believe nobody owes them a thing, but they too often see plenty who think everybody owes them something. They believe freedom is worth fighting for because without it there's little left to live for. But they also believe freedom has been defined by nature, nature's law, and the moral gravity that determines our conduct; therefore, it is never an absolute. And, when evil comes to harm their families or the innocent, then ending its existence is the most agreed upon option… this much, I know they believe.

Thank you.

Thanks for reading this collection of thoughts I worked so hard to get down before they slipped away from me forever. I nearly waited too long to look back. If one waits too long they might forget to say thank you.

I might have allowed time to erode the opportunity if it were not for Jim Edwards. He encouraged me to write this book. I don't think this is exactly what he had in mind, but I hope it's better than his expectation… I don't know. What I do know is that I owe him a thank you. He convinced me that I had something to share and it was worthy of sharing. I really don't know how he did it, we were just shooting on his range one day and he blurted it out… "You need to write a book". I'm still a little perplexed at how when two fellows were sending lead down range this inspiration to write a book arose. Perhaps it was supposed to be a suspense novel and I got a bit confused. Anyway… thanks so very much Jim.

It would be a bit difficult to list the many leaders who played a role in my life, especially the ones from the Teams. A list would be quite comprehensive. I must give the name of my stepfather Jerry Christopher Robertson and my brother Wesley Martin, two seemingly ordinary men with an extraordinary strength for leadership. As for the Teams, I will mention the names of the most influential, much of which occurred early in my career; however, there were a number of others… sounds like an Oscar speech doesn't it? In the order by which they were discovered is, Jim O'Connell, Bob Donegan, Hershel Davis, RJ Thomas, Steve Elson, Pete Irish, and Tom Tarbox. They certainly deserved an Oscar.

What is a book's "thank you" without the mention of one's wife; it's nearly mandatory… sure hope she's laughing. Twenty-nine years and not a single argument… now she's laughing. You're the very best friend Donna, and too often the effort by women such as yourself is overlooked. You should know it has never been overlooked by me; your sacrifices were immensely greater than mine. Collectively we have spent years apart and you've never complained. I certainly hope this wasn't after you helped pack my bags and then following such rushed me from the house. I doubt it! However, I do think you should've at least allowed me to say farewell to our daughters, or perhaps the house pets… now she's pensively humored. You have accused me many times of being less than affectionate; true this might be, but you can never accuse me of not deeply loving you. Unfortunately, no other words exist but "thank you" for your great effort, and even if they did it would be less than deserved. Less than desired but all that I have, and so I thank you! You've proved yourself a wise and wonderful wife, mother, and leader... now comes well-deserved tears.

So it is that a man who had no redeemable attributes as far as I experienced, became the man who seemed to collect them all. Before his faith, I did not hate him but I did not love him either... emotionally neutral. I sincerely didn't care about him in the smallest of ways. If he inspired any emotion in me it was fear, but that gives little to brag about doesn't it? As a child things are so less complicated, but immensely more difficult to comprehend. By the time I was in my adolescent years I had already developed a rather serious unaffectionate nature. Then came an unexplainable explainable, should anyone want to argue the merits of God's enabling salvation then you better bring along some pretty damn convincing evidence. I'm not settling for a discussion but rather something demonstrable because this is what I have. I'm going to expect you to redirect a bolt of lightening; touch the sun with a finger, and just to be sure I would prefer you create your own creature from nothing but dirt... seems reasonable.

I don't know most of the answers but I know much of the experience. How then can a man suddenly be transformed in mere moments? How does a man once a convict of the law suddenly become a convict of faith, but with just a few words spoken by way of a very simple request? How does the difficult weight of his past become the feather of his future at the blink of anyone's eye? And he became an affectionate loving father and husband who displayed an entirely different human than previously experienced. Within a few moments the burden of his past was suddenly left behind.

Forgiveness is powerful, a transformational element that stands completely undisturbed by physical science. I cannot proclaim to be brilliant at it; frankly, I could use significant improvement. However, I thoroughly understand its indispensable virtues. The perfectly irrational, but powerfully rational, life changing strength of forgiveness made an enormous difference and produced a leader in more than the life of just one. Thank you so very much dad; sorry you had to leave so damn early. I certainly wish He'd have reconsidered; He might be easy to speak with but sometimes very hard to convince. In this matter, I was unable to move as much as the described mustard seed with my faith… it needs work for sure, so to hell with the mountain. I gave it my very best prayers dad, this much I promise; you were the very first of my leaders.

I would like to think He's just above my head as though He is always a mere breath away. I can't contemplate heaven from this earth, it seems unimaginably far. I would like to believe my conversations with Him are within the space of my person, because it does me no good to think a contrite "thank you" must be transported within some distance that I cannot express. I prefer to believe He is just above my head, and even though I have unanswered questions I've no doubts. Why then if He were to answer all my questions would I need faith? If I had a depository of all life's questions answered I wouldn't need Him for much; therefore, I really wouldn't have a reason to believe in much. How do I hope for anything better if my belief is given no purpose? Whether you hope for better things on earth or those things in heaven, it requires faith, and only by faith does hope have purpose; I am not discouraged that mine is not better. I know that by following the Leader above, I've been given an opportunity to be a leader below, no matter the size of my contribution... I am given to thank Him... so thanks!